DREAMS AND DEEDS

DREAMS AND DEEDS:
ACHIEVEMENT MOTIVATION
IN NIGERIA

ROBERT A. LeVINE
with the assistance of EUGENE STRANGMAN
and LEONARD UNTERBERGER

THE UNIVERSITY OF CHICAGO PRESS / Chicago and London

Library of Congress Catalog Card Number 66-20580

THE UNIVERSITY OF CHICAGO PRESS, CHICAGO & LONDON
The University of Toronto Press, Toronto 5, Canada

To Nigerian schoolboys and their future
and to the memory of Dorothy Eggan, pioneer
in cross-cultural dream research
this book is dedicated

By picturing our wishes as fulfilled, dreams are after all leading us into the future. But this future, which the dreamer pictures as the present, has been moulded by his indestructible wish into a perfect likeness of the past.

Sigmund Freud, *The Interpretation of Dreams*

ACKNOWLEDGMENTS

The research reported in this book was supported by the National Institutes of Health (Grant M-4865), the Ford Foundation Child Development Project of the University of Ibadan, and the University of Chicago (Committee for the Comparative Study of New Nations under a grant from the Carnegie Corporation of New York and Committee on Near Eastern and African Studies). The analysis and writing of results were done during the senior author's tenure as a recipient of a Research Career Development Award from the National Institute of Mental Health and a Fellow of the Foundations' Fund for Research in Psychiatry.

Thanks are due to the many persons in Nigeria who helped in the collection of the school data. These include: Professor Andrew Taylor, Director of the Institute of Education, University of Ibadan, who made his office and other facilities available and initiated contacts with the schools; B. Lloyd and B. Briggs of the institute staff, who aided in the administration of the instruments; A. H. M. Kirk-Greene of the Institute of Administration, Zaria, and Richard Henderson (now of Yale University), who helped select and communicate with schools in Zaria and Onitsha, respectively; and the principals and teachers of the eight schools in which data were collected — Government College (Ibadan), Ibadan Grammar School, Ibadan Boys' High School, Government College (Zaria), Provincial Secondary School (Zaria), Institute of Administration (Zaria), Dennis Memorial Grammar School (Onitsha), and New Bethel College (Onitsha). Their willing cooperation in a study which promised no immediate results was extremely gratifying.

The data were analyzed at the University of Chicago, where many other persons contributed to the handling of the data, scoring, statistical analysis, and preparation of the manuscript. We wish to express our gratitude to Carl O'Nell, Constance Rae Fries, Annette Elvove, and Beverly Esenwein for their indispensable help.

The senior author gratefully acknowledges his special intellectual debts to those who helped inform or challenge him concerning the subject matter of this study: to Norman M. Bradburn, who fired his interest in achievement motivation; to Robin Horton and John Whiting, who fruitfully disagreed with him concerning Ibo-Yoruba differences; to Peter Lloyd, Akin Mabogunje, Richard and Helen Henderson, and Gloria Marshall for many informative discussions on the Yoruba and Ibo as they had known them in their own field work; to his colleagues on the Committee for the Comparative Study of New Nations, who reacted to an initial presentation of the results contained herein; and to Donald T. Campbell, whose strategy of science influenced the analysis and discussion of the findings of this study. Helpful comments on a first draft of the manuscript were received from Richard Henderson, Alex Inkeles, S. Gillmore Lee, David C. McClelland, M. G. Smith, and Fred L. Strodtbeck. We are thankful to all, but particularly to Professor Lee for his many concrete suggestions. The responsibility for the study as here presented, however, lies entirely with the authors.

R. A. L.
E. S.
L. U.

CONTENTS

TABLES

1

INTRODUCTION

It has become increasingly clear that a high rate of economic development in a country cannot be guaranteed by the presence of abundant natural resources, capital, and even skilled manpower. Consequently, serious attention has been paid to the suggestion that psychological, and particularly motivational, factors may be importantly involved.

PSYCHOLOGICAL FACTORS IN ECONOMIC DEVELOPMENT

The "psychological position" is that an individual drive to excel is required for the entrepreneurial activity which converts resources, capital, and manpower into production and — eventually — income. Where this drive is strong and widespread in a population, the economy will develop rapidly through the cumulative push of entrepreneurial actions; where the drive is weak or infrequent, economic advance will be slow. Proponents of this psychological position attribute differences in the rate of economic growth, between the "have" and "have-not" nations and between rapidly industrializing nations like Japan and those countries which have lagged behind, to corresponding differences in the incidence of this drive to excel among the national populations concerned. Particular ethnic groups specializing in trade have been singled out as having more of this motive than do their neighbors within some of the underdeveloped countries. Thus a psychological factor — an acquired drive for excellence or need to achieve — is held to be unevenly distributed in the human species and to be at least partly responsible for the major national and other group differences in economic growth which are so conspicuous in the contemporary world.

In this study we are concerned not with national differences but

1

with the uneven distribution of achievement motivation among the ethnic groups of a major African nation. In areas like Africa, where new political boundaries and state organization have been super-imposed on peoples of diverse language and tradition, inequalities in the capacity of these component peoples to take advantage of the opportunities offered by nationhood and modernization can have far-reaching social and political consequences. Vast new avenues of advancement have been opened up by independent self-govern-ment, the expansion of educational opportunities, and the effort to end visible economic domination by foreigners. Those groups whose members are best prepared to take advantage of these op-portunities are likely to attain a position of dominance in the civil service, business management, the professions, intellectual and ar-tistic circles, and generally in the class of Western-educated persons who tend to be so influential in predominantly illiterate societies. In other words, such groups are likely to form a disproportionate segment of the modernized governing elite in the nation and thus to create an ethnic basis for possible antagonism between traditional and modern, or even between privileged and underprivileged, ele-ments in the population. The conspicuous success of one group may generate intense and potentially disruptive competition between ethnic groups over access to opportunities and the allocation of positions of influence. On the other hand, ethnically unbalanced achievements may lead the less successful group to attempt changes in their mode of life. The general and obvious importance of rela-tions between ethnic groups in these societies endows with unusual significance any demonstrable differences in the capacities of their members to control social and economic resources.

In contemporary Africa the rise of certain ethnic groups noted for energy, achievement striving, and enterprise has been remarked by many local and foreign observers. The Kikuyu in Kenya, the Chagga in Tanganyika, the Ewe in Ghana, the Bamileke in Came-roun, and the Ibo in Nigeria are examples of groups noted for their opportunism and industry in response to the new situation created by Western institutions in this century. Although none of these groups forms an electoral majority in its nation, most have become major forces to be reckoned with, through dominance, dissidence, or some complicated combination of the two, and they seem likely to retain this status for a long time. These intranational differences in enterprise and actual achievement play a part in shaping the course of political events and social development in post-colonial Africa, their relevance to national integration being particularly important. The nature of the societies which emerge from the rapid changes of recent years will depend in part on the differential economic and educational advancement of the various ethnic groups which comprise them. Are these differential rates and patterns of advancement related to motivational differences between the culturally diverse populations? This is a question we seek to answer for three ethnic groups in Nigeria.

AFRICAN ATTITUDES TOWARD WORK AND ACHIEVEMENT

Variations in achievement among African groups can be properly understood only against the background of attitudes toward work and achievement which are extremely widespread, if not universal, in Africa. It must first of all be understood that few African populations fit the stereotype of the conservative, fatalistic peasant tenaciously clinging to a traditional way of life and content to continue the annual cycle without hope of improvement for himself or his descendants in this world. In nearly all traditional African societies with which we are acquainted, the pecuniary motive was well developed, and competition for wealth, prestige, and political power was frequent and intense. Individuals did strive to better their lot and that of their children, and in many parts of the continent they came quickly to see the possibilities for advancement in the trade patterns, schools, and bureaucratic institutions introduced by Europeans. Compared with folk and peasant peoples in other parts of the world, Africans have been unusually responsive to economic incentives and Western education. The aspirations of even remote villagers for material improvement and their passion for schooling seems remarkable to a foreign visitor. Rather than thinking of Africans as tradition-directed people perpetuating an ancient and stagnant culture, we might more accurately regard them as pragmatic frontiersmen with a persistent history of migration, settlement and resettlement of new lands, and of responding to the challenges of intertribal wars and the slave trade. In this historical perspective Africans were experienced in adapting to and taking advantage of change, instability, and movement, so that they were more prepared to adopt new paths of advancement offered by European institutions than were the populations of some of the more stable non-Western societies.

The frontiersman image does not, however, adequately convey the most widespread African attitude toward work. Africans aspire to wealth and status — in new as well as old forms — and many of them are also industrious farmers, craftsmen, and professionals, but they do not generally regard hard work as highly commendable in itself. On the contrary, their traditional status systems present extreme examples of what Thorstein Veblen called "conspicuous leisure" [1] — that is, the social pattern in which freedom from work is a prerogative of high status and is publicly displayed in order to reinforce one's position. Although conspicuous leisure is a feature of all societies, in Africa it is found at all levels of society in forms of status defined by sex, age, wealth, and political office, and is organized around the high evaluation put on commanding persons of a lower status to perform tasks that the superordinate person might perform himself. It is by demonstration of the power to command the labor of others that a person maintains his status in the public eye. Hence a man of eminence who performs a menial task for himself out of necessity, desire for efficiency, or perfectionism is not regarded as praiseworthy but as having demeaned himself socially. His neighbors would begin to say that he had lost the respect of his subordinates and could no longer order them about. In some African societies ordinary persons are so protective of the public status of the relatively eminent that they rush to relieve the latter of demeaning tasks, thereby also ingratiating themselves.

It must be emphasized that although the most elaborated forms of conspicuous leisure in Africa are associated with monarchies and deference to royal personages (as they are elsewhere), the pattern is found widely diffused throughout society without rigid caste or class divisions. An East African local chief or a West African wealthy trader will be surrounded by lackeys to attend to every task he or his family might want performed, and many of these lackeys will be his own kinsmen rather than persons of a social stratum particularly trained to servitude. The social value assigned to having such assistance is emphasized by the fact that such servants are often recognized by their master as being inefficient or untrustworthy but are considered preferable in that state to his doing without them. A similar situation obtains within the domestic group, where status lines are primarily those of sex and age. Men may be stronger than women, but a man is most likely to have his wife carry a heavy load on her head, even if he is going to the same place, so that he may walk in unencumbered dignity. Small children may be weak, ignorant, and careless, but they are often called upon to carry, clean, or purchase things which adults could do more easily. Highly respected elders are usually granted the authority to demand small services of any man or woman, although the demands are often passed on to younger persons. As Western schooling has progressed, teachers and other educated persons have joined the

[1] Thorstein Veblen, *The Theory of the Leisure Class* (New York: Random House, 1915).

ranks of community notables whose high status both enables them to order others about and requires them to do so. School teachers regularly use their pupils as unpaid domestic servants and even agricultural laborers. Their kinsmen send them children to perform tasks in exchange for the opportunity of being exposed to their educational influences.

To estimate the impact of this kind of status system on the individual, it is necessary to view it from a developmental perspective. The three- or four-year-old is at the very bottom of the domestic status hierarchy; adults and older siblings may pass menial and boring tasks on to him, but he has no one below him to pass them on to. Consequently, he is at anyone's beck and call, and runs errands for his parents, elder siblings, and other adults.[2] As he grows older, he acquires younger siblings or other relatives whom he can order about to some extent, thus relieving himself of some of the more onerous chores. He comes to view growing up as a process of progressive relief from menial tasks and of increasing authority to pass these tasks on to others. Maturity increases a man's status, and higher status means getting others to do things for him. The child's acquisition of these values regarding work and status may also come from his perception of everyday life in the family; whereas in European and American farm families a child is likely to see his father as the hardest-working person in the environment, the African rural child most often sees his father as the person with the most leisure and the women of the house as the hardest-working persons. Since the women are also clearly of lower status, the child is not encouraged to regard work and status as positively correlated. Furthermore, the procedure of ordering those lower in the family hierarchy to do work a person does not relish himself becomes clear to the child at an early age as the proper way of using authority over others. Thus his own developmental experience in the family environment and his perception of it conspire jointly to teach the

[2] The attitude associated with this behavior is illustrated by the following summary of reports from thirty-seven diverse Ghanaian communities as to why people want to have children: "Children are valued for many reasons. Those most often given are: (i) they perform domestic tasks, such as helping in the preparation of food, gathering firewood, sweeping the rooms and the compound, washing the dishes, looking after smaller siblings and running errands; (ii) they are a source of labor on the farm, and assist their fathers in fishing and other occupations; . . . (iii) they enable proper courtesy and respect to be shown to important visitors, by serving and waiting on them; (iv) they uphold their father's dignity in public by carrying his stool and other possessions, and by running errands for him." (Barrington Kaye, *Bringing Up Children in Ghana: An Impressionistic Survey* [London: Allen and Unwin, 1962], p. 24.)

child that increasing status inevitably entails relative freedom from work at the expense of his subordinates.

This pattern of experience and the resultant internalization of status values may help to account for the subsequent behavior of many Africans in modern employment situations, particularly bureaucratic ones. In contemporary Africa the employed person — and especially the civil servant — is several social degrees above the rural folk with whom he was raised. In accordance with the values he has acquired, he expresses the difference in status through conspicuous leisure and the use of subordinates in his domestic life and on his visits home. If he attempted to apply these same patterns in his employment situation, however, he would be in opposition to Western-derived standards of bureaucratic behavior. Thus the African civil servant is often accused by Western observers of too great reliance on incompetent subordinates to get jobs done rather than doing them himself, as well as of being relatively unresponsive to the legitimate requests of low-status applicants for service. We believe that such bureaucrats have a need to reaffirm their positions as relatively high-status persons by demonstrating that they have messengers and other assistants to do their bidding and that they are not at the beck and call of lowly citizens. Such needs may be stronger than the need to demonstrate efficiency. Furthermore, lacking in their own family backgrounds the image of a hard-working person of high social status, African civil servants may feel a loss rather than a gain in self-esteem at the prospect of putting in a hard day's work, especially if his work does not involve directing others. Self-reliant task performance in a non-administrative position, regarded as highly commendable in the West, is seen by the African clerk as depriving him of his only opportunity to attain job satisfaction according to his own standards.

This generalized analysis of African work attitudes may help to eliminate some of the confusion regarding ambition and achievement in African societies which many Western observers have experienced. As mentioned above, the high ambitions or aspirations of Africans are striking to the foreign observer, who becomes quickly aware of their desire for education and their competition for jobs and other means of acquiring wealth and position. All this seems very Western. African concepts of how to attain success and of how to behave in positions of responsibility, however, differ considerably from those current in the West. The point of greatest contrast is self-reliance, since the Western ideal of achieving excellence on a person's own runs counter to the African notion that self-reliance involves displaying a humiliating lack of social power. Many employed Africans overtly subscribe to Western achievement goals, but they are by no means willing to risk the loss of prestige resulting from refusing the prerogatives of their positions. Furthermore, they believe — often correctly — that they are more likely to attain success through a clever manipulation of their subordinates and superiors than through self-reliant effort. Thus it happens that Africans and Westerners use the same language of achievement, competition, success, and even hard work, but mean by these terms quite different patterns of behavior.

ETHNIC GROUPS IN CONTEMPORARY NIGERIA

There have been no previous systematic studies of achievement motivation in Africa. Nigeria was a natural choice for the first such study, especially one concentrating on intranational differences, since it contains within its population (the largest in Africa) groups which vary drastically on numerous social and cultural dimensions, including Westernization. Furthermore, despite the existence there of more than two hundred ethnic-linguistic units, the life of the nation is dominated to a large extent by the three largest ethnic groups, the Hausa, the Yoruba, and the Ibo, whose separate destinies and relations with each other are central to the future development of the Federation of Nigeria.

These three ethnic groups differ culturally, and each plays a unique role in contemporary Nigeria. From the viewpoint of Lagos, the national capital, a brief summary of these roles might be something like the following.

The Hausa are the "backwoods" politicians: conservative, religiously orthodox (Islam), with little formal education or urban sophistication, but with the largest bloc of votes in their control and a well-developed sense of practical power politics. They have been politically dominant in the federation, owing to the vast, largely illiterate and politically inert population of Northern Nigeria they control; but they are almost unrepresented in the educated elite of the country, on whom they must depend in many aspects of government.

The Yoruba are the most urbane group, with the longest history of Westernization, Christianity, and education. They include the patrician families of Lagos, as well as the earliest members of nearly every profession and department of the civil service, in which they are still strong. If there was an "establishment" of Nigerians in high position during the colonial period, it was largely that of the Yoruba, who gave to the capital city of Lagos (an indigenous Yoruba town) that combination of Victorian respectability and the spend-thrift pursuit of pleasure which colors its elite culture to this day.

The Ibo are the energetic parvenus who in a few decades altered the established order, both by successfully challenging Yoruba supremacy in the professional and civil service elite and by leading the struggle for Nigerian nationalism which led to independence from Britain. Although the Ibo have generated the greatest number of political militants and radicals, their politicians realistically entered into a coalition with the Hausa which ruled the country from 1959 to 1965. In the latter year, members of the Yoruba Nigerian National Democratic Party were taken into the cabinet, and on January 15, 1966, a group of Ibo army officers overthrew the government and upset the ethnic alignment of power. With a level of ideological, constitutional, and pragmatic sophistication which is rare among the new nations of Africa, Nigerian politics are not simply a reflection of tribal divisions, and are therefore capable of coalitions and cleavages which are not easily predictable from knowledge of the ethnic groups and their differences. Nonetheless, the fact remains that ethnic loyalties are strong and that a major part of Nigerian social, economic, and political development is dependent on the activities of Hausa, Ibo, and Yoruba, who seem to outside observers (and each other) very different kinds of people.

These ethnic divergences have been most incisively examined by Coleman, whose treatment of them in his comprehensive sociopolitical history of colonial Nigeria suggested the specific hypotheses for the present study. The following quotations indicate how far toward psychological questions the political scientist was pushed in his attempt to understand the factors accounting for the particular pattern of economic and political development in Nigeria.

Tribal response to impact of modern economic forces has been highly varied in Nigeria, not only because of geographical, topographical, and historical differences, or of variations in the distribution of resources . . . but also because of cultural differences in the capacity and predisposition of different groups and subgroups to adapt to the new forces.

These cultural differences have been determined in part by the traditional social structure and the degree of upward mobility within that structure, the attitudes toward property and toward wealth individually acquired, and the relationship between wealth and political power. In traditional Ibo society, for example, there was much upward mobility and a fairly close correlation between the individual acquisition of wealth and the exercise of legitimate political power. In Hausa society a very different cultural pattern prevailed. Again, one finds further cultural variations, such as Yoruba youths refusing to turn to wage labor if it involved being a servant, Hausa traders finding clerkship unattractive. . . . These tribal variations are significant because they have partly determined the tribal composition of the commercialized and economically involved elements.[3]

Another factor of indeterminate significance in the Ibo awakening was certain characteristic personality and behavioral traits attributed to this group. Some observers have sought to relate such traits to distinctive patterns of Ibo culture. M. M. Green points out that "it is the 'go-getter' who is admired, the man who has wives and children and bestirs himself and makes money. . . . A man who just sits quiet is not respected." Life in some traditional Ibo societies tends to be highly competitive, and great stress is placed upon achieved status. Some of these traits are particularly characteristic of the Aro, a subgroup within Ibo society. Fanning out from Arochuku, their homeland, the Aro, by shrewdness, strong familial bonds, and hard work, acquired substantial influence in many Ibo towns where Aro colonies were formed. These facts are, of course, very suggestive, but generalizations about "national character" and culturally determined behavioral traits must be treated with great caution. Competitiveness, materialism, and emphasis upon achieved status are not unique with the Ibo, nor necessarily common to all Ibo. At the very highest level of generalization and comparison, however, they are traits that gave birth to certain national stereotypes and provided a basis for distinguishing the attitudes and behavior of the typical Ibo from those of the typical Yoruba or Hausa. But even here a distinction would have to be made between generations, as second and third generation Yoruba and Hausa youths have been less affected by traditional cultural determinants.[4]

These observations go as far as scientific caution allows in describing group personality characteristics and in relating them to traditional social structures on the basis of ethnographic and historical impressions. The present study uses the methods of social psychology in an attempt to test these notions.

[3] James S. Coleman, *Nigeria: Background to Nationalism* (Berkeley and Los Angeles: University of California Press, 1958), p. 64.
[4] *Ibid.*, pp. 333–35.

2

SOCIAL STRUCTURE,
PERSONALITY,
AND ACHIEVEMENT

This study of ethnic differences in Nigeria is aimed not only at furthering the systematic knowledge of African social behavior but also at helping to answer three general and fundamental questions in the field of psychological anthropology. Are there objectively measurable differences in personality between culturally differing populations? If so, what are the sociocultural causes of such differences? What are the social consequences of these differences? In this comparison of the Hausa, Ibo, and Yoruba, we attempt to deal with these questions in the context of one specific personality characteristic — achievement motivation; one specific sociocultural determinant — the status mobility system; and one particular social consequence — attitudes and behaviors relevant to economic development.

CONCEPTS OF PERSONALITY AND SOCIAL STRUCTURE

The basic hypothesis of this study stems from a general proposition implicit or explicit in statements concerning personality and social structure made by numerous sociologists (from Durkheim and W. I. Thomas onward), anthropologists, psychologists, and psychoanalysts: that inasmuch as societies can be maintained only through the willing conformity of individuals to social norms, there must be some kind of "fit" between the personality characteristics (or behavioral dispositions) of individuals in a society and the social structures within which they function. If this is true, it should be possible to find in comparative study concomitant variations between personality characteristics and structural characteristics —

across societies if the societies are relatively stable, or over time if the societies are changing.

There are, however, two divergent views on the nature of the personality characteristics which co-vary with social structure. One position, most explicitly presented in the works of Inkeles,[1] is that correspondences should be found between specific role requirements in the social system and specific personality traits of individuals who must fill these roles. For example, a society with an authoritarian structure of political roles should be found to have in its population many individuals of authoritarian disposition, as measured independently of their required role performance. The mediating factor is ideology, which not only permeates the structure, setting standards for adequate role performance, but also influences the training and selection of individuals for social roles.

The other position, formulated by Parsons and Shils [2] and Spiro,[3] is clearly stated by Kaplan:

> Social and personality systems need not be symmetrical or isomorphically structured. A small number of different motivations may support a wide variety of different behaviors, or quite diverse motivations in different persons may be the basis for the same role behavior. Since either can be the case, motivations are emancipated from role requirements and we are forced to seek a new conception of the relationship between the two. . . .
> We must no longer think of the motivation of a great variety of diverse behaviors but of a single diffuse disposition or orientation. Instead of positing for each specific behavior of the person — i.e., aggressive behavior, affiliative behavior — its own motivation, we must be concerned with discovering the motivations that underlie the generalized mechanism, conformity.[4]

Kaplan views the conformative dispositions of the individual as the only part of his personality which is directly relevant to social structure and likely to co-vary with it. He offers Riesman's [5] cate-

---

[1] Alex Inkeles, "Personality and Social Structure," in *Sociology Today*, ed. R. K. Merton, L. Broom, and L. S. Cottrell (New York: Basic Books, 1959); "Sociology and Psychology," in *Psychology: Study of a Science*, VI, ed. S. Koch (New York: McGraw-Hill, 1963); with Daniel J. Levinson, "National Character," in *Handbook of Social Psychology*, ed. G. Lindzey (Cambridge, Mass.: Addison-Wesley, 1954).

[2] Talcott Parsons and Edward Shils, *Toward a General Theory of Action* (Cambridge, Mass.: Harvard University Press, 1951), p. 152.

[3] Melford E. Spiro, "Social Systems, Personality, and Functional Analysis," in *Studying Personality Cross-Culturally*, ed. B. Kaplan (Evanston, Ill.: Row Peterson, 1961).

[4] Bert Kaplan, "Editor's Epilogue," in *Studying Personality Cross-Culturally*, ed. B. Kaplan (Evanston, Ill.: Row Peterson, 1961), pp. 663–67.

[5] David Riesman, *The Lonely Crowd* (New Haven: Yale University Press, 1950).

gories of social character (tradition-directed, inner-directed, other-directed) as examples of "different psychological bases for a conformative relationship to social norms." [6]

The orientation of the present study is closer to the first position, in which specific correspondences between individual motivation and socially structured role requirements are predicted. We view the social system as a selective, normative environment which exerts pressures in favor of those personality traits which facilitate optimal performance in social roles. Such pressures, operating through socializing agents who influence the developing individual, act to skew the distribution of personality traits in the population toward the socially valued norms for role performance. Thus societies whose social systems have differed for several generations are expected to vary concomitantly in the relative frequency with which some psychological characteristics appear in their populations. This position is stated in more detail below as it applies to status mobility and achievement motivation.

ETHNIC VARIATIONS IN
ACHIEVEMENT MOTIVATION

No social motive has been more thoroughly studied than the need for achievement, commonly referred to by psychologists as *n* Achievement.[7] The term is defined as a latent disposition to compete with a standard of excellence, and involves both a persistent desire for such competition and an emotional concern with it. It is assumed that the motive is expressed by the individual as affective concern about, or preoccupation with: doing well in relation to achievement goals, unique accomplishment, long-term commitment to the attainment of such goals, instrumental acts directed toward their attainment, obstacles to be overcome, and prospects of success or failure. Operationally, the presence of any of these elements in fantasies produced by individuals is taken as indicative of *n* Achievement. The usual method of measuring the motive used by McClelland and his colleagues and students is to analyze the content of stories produced in reaction to a series of pictures from the Thematic Apperception Test (TAT), but a similar system of analysis has been applied to a variety of other individual and group fantasy productions. In experimental situations in several societies it has been demonstrated that when subjects are told that their per-

[6] Kaplan, *op. cit.*, p. 666.

[7] Cf. David C. McClelland, *The Achieving Society* (Princeton: Van Nostrand, 1961).

formance will be evaluated they produce TAT stories with significantly more n Achievement than when they are given neutral instructions.[8] The n Achievement scores of individuals have been shown to be correlated with a variety of overt response measures, which involve active striving to do well, delay of gratification, and preference for moderate risk taking.[9] These behaviors are seen by McClelland as adaptive in the performance of entrepreneurial roles, so that, other things being equal, men with high n Achievement are better suited to entrepreneurial roles and are more likely to devote themselves to doing well in numerous spheres of activity. A greater frequency of men high in n Achievement in a population will lead, according to McClelland, to a higher level of economic growth and other forms of cultural achievement.[10]

Several studies using the TAT measure of n Achievement have shown statistically significant differences between groups of individuals drawn from culturally divergent societies. For example, United States subjects manifested higher n Achievement scores than comparable groups of Brazilian[11] and Turkish[12] subjects, the differences in both instances being significant at the .001 level of probability. Ethnic groups within the United States have been shown to differ on mean n Achievement scores, with Greek, Jewish, and white Protestant subjects scoring relatively high, Italian subjects scoring intermediate, and French-Canadian and Negro subjects scoring low.[13] Such rankings of ethnic groups on achievement motivation are roughly consistent with their respective rates of movement into high-status occupations, although there are many confounding factors which prevent precise comparability. In the United States,[14] Brazil,[15] and Japan,[16] social class differences in average level of achievement motivation are pronounced, with a general tendency for higher-status groups to score higher, although the highest scores are usually found among the upper-middle classes rather than the highest class. These findings, taken as a whole, indicate that there are differences in achievement motivation between groups

[8] *Ibid.*, pp. 39–43.
[9] *Ibid.*, pp. 43–46.
[10] *Ibid.*, pp. 46–57. This is the basic proposition of the entire volume by McClelland, and it is discussed in many other places within the book.
[11] Bernard C. Rosen, "Socialization and Achievement Motivation in Brazil," *American Sociological Review*, XXVII, No. 5 (1962), p. 623.
[12] Norman M. Bradburn, "N Achievement and Father Dominance in Turkey," *Journal of Abnormal and Social Psychology*, LXVII, No. 5 (1963), p. 466.
[13] McClelland, *op. cit.*, p. 362.
[14] *Ibid.*, pp. 362–63.
[15] Rosen, *op. cit.*, p. 623.
[16] McClelland, *op. cit.*, p. 379.

defined on a cultural or ethnic basis, and that within socially stratified societies there is a relationship between social status and n Achievement.

McClelland and his associates have carried out a number of historical and cross-cultural studies in which they scored the literature or oral narratives of societies for n Achievement.[17] But the study of group fantasy most relevant to the present investigation is that of Parker.[18] In a comparison of the ethnographic evidence on the Eskimo and Ojibwa, Parker concluded that the Ojibwa strove for individual achievement and power and were highly competitive, independent, and suspicious of one another, whereas the Eskimo were much more cooperative and put less emphasis on individual achievement and the acquisition of power. On this basis he predicted that in comparable samples of fantasy from the two groups, the Ojibwa would manifest a higher level of achievement and power motivation, whereas the Eskimo would show more of the affiliation motive. A random sample of twenty-nine myths was chosen from published collections for each of the societies and was scored for n Achievement, n Power, and n Affiliation, according to an adaptation of the TAT scoring system, by a psychologist who had no knowledge of the hypotheses or the cultures. The findings were in striking concordance with prediction. Although Parker's study cannot be said to have proved anything conclusively, it represents a promising indication of a relationship between the social behavior of a people as manifested in standard ethnographic evidence and their social motives as measured independently through the psychological analysis of fantasy. Furthermore, as contrasted with the studies of group differences cited above, it indicates a difference in the level of achievement motivation between two autonomous groups in the same region who are at approximately the same level of economic development.

What causes group differences in achievement motivation? McClelland has distinguished between "intrinsic" determinants, which are required to produce n Achievement in the individual, and "extrinsic" factors, which operate to bring about the individual conditions under which n Achievement is produced.[19] The most widely accepted theory, backed by considerable evidence, indicates that child-rearing or socialization practices are the most important intrinsic factors. Rosen summarizes the evidence as follows:

[17] *Ibid.*, pp. 63–158.

[18] Seymour Parker, "Motives in Eskimo and Ojibwa Mythology," *Ethnology*, I, No. 4 (1962), pp. 516–23.

[19] McClelland, *op. cit.*, pp. 337–40.

Several studies have shown that achievement motivation has its origin in a complex of inter-related socialization practices. The first and most important of these is *achievement training*. Parents who provide this type of training set high goals for their child, indicate a high evaluation of his competence to do a task well, and impose standards of excellence upon problem-solving tasks, even in situations where such standards are not explicit. Also related to the development of achievement motivation is another set of socialization practices called *independence training*. This type of training involves expectations that the child be *self-reliant* when competing with standards of excellence. At the same time the child is granted *autonomy* in problem-solving and decision-making in situations where he has both freedom of action and responsibility for success or failure. Essentially, achievement training is concerned with getting the child to do things well, while independence training seeks to teach him to do things on his own (self-reliance) in a situation where he enjoys relative freedom from parental control (autonomy).[20]

Studies conducted in Brazil, Japan, and Germany indicate that achievement demands made by mothers at the age of eight are more likely to produce high *n* Achievement than such demands made earlier or later.[21] In addition to these specific dimensions of training, aspects of family structure (considered "extrinsic" by McClelland) have been shown to be involved in the development of *n* Achievement. The optimal pattern for producing *n* Achievement seems to be: a somewhat dominating mother who emphasizes standards of excellence, and a father who allows his son autonomy. The authoritarian, father-dominated family is less likely to produce men high in achievement motivation, as Rosen has argued in his study of Brazil.[22] Where the family *is* father-dominated, as in Turkey, men who had lived apart from their families from an early age manifested higher *n* Achievement than those raised in intact families.[23] Also, families which use servants or slaves in the raising of children, by lowering the demands for self-reliance and achievement, are less likely to produce men high in *n* Achievement.[24] Thus achievement motivation is seen as fostered by a pre-adolescent environment consisting of a particular pattern of adult-child relationships and training experiences.

The "extrinsic" factors most emphasized by McClelland are the ideological convictions of parents which lead them to modify their child-rearing practices in the direction of those described above as optimal for the development of *n* Achievement.[25] If the parents

[20] Rosen, *op. cit.*, p. 612.
[21] McClelland, *op. cit.*, pp. 345–47.
[22] Rosen, *op. cit.*, pp. 623–24.
[23] Bradburn, *op. cit.*, p. 467.
[24] Cf. McClelland, *op. cit.*, pp. 376–78.
[25] *Ibid.*, pp. 356–57.

strongly adopt an ideology stressing individualism and self-reliance, they will attempt to promote these qualities in their children through intense training in independence and self-reliance. Thus McClelland adds to Weber's hypothesis that Protestantism led to the spirit of modern capitalism by asserting that it did so through the mediation of the child-rearing practices of Protestant parents which produced generations of men high in *n* Achievement who actively engaged in entrepreneurial activity.[26] Religious ideologies of "positive mysticism," in which each individual can approach God directly but in which the world is not renounced, are hypothesized to have this effect on parental values and practices which in turn lead to worldly success. Besides Calvinists, the Quakers, Jains, Hindu Vaishnavas, Zen Buddhists, and Hassidic Jews are offered as examples.[27] In a cross-cultural study of forty-five nonliterate societies, McClelland shows a strong association between emphasis on individual (as opposed to ritual) contact with the divine and *n* Achievement in folktales.[28] Other extrinsic factors are considered, but, apart from family structure itself (as in the presence and authority position of the father and the use of servants or slaves in child rearing), religious ideology is taken as the single most powerful sociocultural determinant of achievement training and motivation whose effect can be demonstrated.

This compressed review of the literature on ethnic variations in achievement motivation and their alleged causes shows the strongly psychological orientation of those who have investigated the subject. Beginning with variations in motivational level, they have worked back toward the determinants of these variations in child rearing and parental values and forward to the effects of these variations on entrepreneurial role behavior and economic development. Generally (Parker's study being a limited exception) the social structure, apart from patterns of family interaction, has not been seen as exercising an independent determinate influence on the level of *n* Achievement in the population. This brings us to the theoretical background of the present investigation.

A THEORY OF STATUS MOBILITY
AND ACHIEVEMENT MOTIVATION

We stated above that a social structure can be seen as a normative environment exerting selective pressures that affect the distribution of personality traits in a population. Here our attention

[26] *Ibid.*, pp. 46–50.
[27] *Ibid.*, pp. 367–70.
[28] *Ibid.*, pp. 370–72.

is confined to the status system and its impact on the frequencies of *n* Achievement and related personality traits in a population.

Each system of ranked statuses in which mobility is possible from one status to another constitutes in effect an allocation of social rewards for some types of behavior — those which make for upward movement. These rewarded types of behavior can be and are perceived as qualities of persons, the kind of person who is likely to rise in a given status mobility system. Thus each status mobility system generates an "ideal personality type" — that is, a normatively buttressed image of the successful man, which is widely held by the population or at least those segments of it for whom mobility is possible.[29] This image is part of the ideology of a status system, and insofar as the status system is actually legitimate — that is, accepted as the right order of things by the population — adults in that population will be imbued with that ideology. The status values inherent in the system will be their values, and the normative image of the successful man will serve as their catalogue of admirable qualities to foster in those who come under their tutelage. Insofar as such encouragement is successful (a point we discuss below), it will result in increasing the frequency in the population of those traits regarded as facilitating status mobility.

A hypothetical contrast will serve to illustrate. Suppose that one society has a status system in which a person from the lower orders can rise only by first becoming the lackey of a high-status person and then by showing himself to be utterly loyal, obedient, and useful to his patron, who eventually rewards the lackey with the riches, positions, and power he has at his disposal. In such a society, obedience and servility are likely to be regarded as virtues — personal qualities which help a man to rise socially and gain access to the resources of the world. Parents, teachers, and adults in other instructional situations (for example, the master-apprentice or employer-employee relationships) will seek to foster these virtues in the young through early and intense obedience training, direct tuition in respect and flattery behavior, punishment for tendencies which might result in antagonizing superiors, and the like. The products of such a socialization process will probably include a larger proportion of individuals high in personality traits such as compliance and deference than would a group of their counterparts in a population less imbued with the ideology of sycophancy. By contrast, imagine another society in which status mobility is managed largely through outstanding performance in an occupational role, where it is possible for someone of humble origins to attain

[29] C.f. Lloyd Fallers, "Equality, Modernity, and Democracy in the New States," in *Old Societies and New States*, ed. C. Geertz (Glencoe, Ill.: The Free Press, 1963), p. 163.

higher status through his own efforts as an independent producer of goods and services or as a broker who marshals social resources for desired ends. Here it is the personal qualities of independence, initiative, industriousness, foresight, and some daring which lead to success and which are considered important virtues to instil in the young through self-reliance and achievement training. The result is likely to be a larger proportion of individuals high in n Achievement than in the first society. Thus a status mobility system, by favoring one set of personal qualities over another, will affect the frequency of relevant personality traits in the population. The strength of this effect is probably contingent on two other factors: the proportion of the total status distance recognized in the society which an individual can traverse in his own lifetime; and the ratio of high-status positions open to the number of potential competitors. In other words, if the rewards of status mobility are high enough and enough of them are available, then the qualities which facilitate status mobility are more likely to be promoted as virtues in a population.

McClelland has characterized the type of theoretical formulation presented here as "a Social Darwinist position of arguing that the social environment inevitably tends to produce the character structure or motivational level 'best' adapted to it."[30] His criticism is that "To assume that they (societies) would generally know how to produce the qualities in their children that they realize are necessary is to take a Social Darwinist or functionalist point of view that gives parents everywhere the credit for knowing more psychology than even those modern psychologists who have studied the problem in detail."[31]

From the mechanistic and empirical viewpoint which we share with McClelland, the major weakness of Social Darwinism is the flaw it has in common with other teleological theories — that of making "purpose" a sufficient explanation of hypothesized relationships, thereby omitting the specification of causal links. If, however, plausible causal links between independently measurable variables can be specified, the theory is no less respectable scientifically than any other untested set of hypotheses.

Our theory involves the following causal chain: status mobility system → parental values (that is, a concept of the ideal successful man) → child-rearing practices → personality frequencies (for example, percentage of population members high in n Achievement or obedience-compliance dispositions). The only point at which this hypothetical framework departs from that of McClelland is in

[30] *Ibid.*, p. 379.
[31] *Ibid.*, p. 383.

the first variable, which is social structural rather than part of a system of religious beliefs. McClelland says, "From the very beginning we have been assuming that parental values as represented in their religious world view would affect child rearing practices and therefore *n* Achievement level."[32] Is it any less plausible to assume that parental values can be represented by the consensus surrounding a well-established, legitimated, status mobility system? We hold that it is not, on the grounds that a status mobility system similarly generates an environment of values concerning the ideal behavior of men in their worldly activities. If an individualistic concept of man's relation to God can be seen as leading parents to emphasize self-reliance and achievement training in their child-rearing practices, it would seem no less reasonable to consider parents as pushed in the same direction by their participation in an adult society in which major social rewards are given to those who do best on their own in competition with a standard of excellence. In both instances it is a matter of an adult applying in his role as parent (or other type of socializing agent) criteria of conduct derived from a general value orientation to which he subscribes as a member of a social group outside the family. The argument linking status mobility values to child-rearing practices is consistent with the reasoning used by Kohn, who accounts for social class differences in United States child rearing in terms of values generated by the father's occupational role.[33] If parents in a complex society can be influenced in their child-rearing practices by criteria of conduct stemming from standards of adequate role performance operative in class-appropriate (working-class and middle-class) occupations, parents in a more homogeneous society may well be so influenced by the system of status mobility in which nearly all participate, directly or indirectly, and to which all give support.

In traditional African and other folk or nonliterate societies, the connection between the status system and child training may be more direct than we are familiar with in the West. This is due to the early — that is, pre-adolescent — induction of children into serious occupational and domestic tasks. Barry, Child, and Bacon found in a large sample of nonliterate societies that those with subsistence economies based on hunting and gathering stressed self-reliance and achievement training more in childhood, whereas those practicing agricultural and animal husbandry laid greater stress on obedience and responsibility.[34] These findings indicate that parents

---

[32] *Ibid.*, p. 356.

[33] Melvin L. Kohn, "Social Class and Parent-Child Relationships: An Interpretation," *American Journal of Sociology*, LXVIII, (1963), pp. 471–80.

[34] H. Barry, I. L. Child, and M. K. Bacon, "Relation of Child Training to Subsistence Economy," *American Anthropologist*, LXI, (1959), pp. 51–63.

in those societies perceive a connection between adult occupational roles and childhood activities which can serve as practice and preparation. Beyond such simulative preparation, Africans begin performing actual adult agricultural and craft work, in the domestic economy and through apprenticeship, while still children. They are thus fully inducted before adolescence into activities which might lead to status mobility. Furthermore, such induction is not limited to roles in economic production: in Buganda, for example, boys served as pages in the courts of kings and chiefs, thus entering the political system of that monarchy. Parallels to this practice existed in other African societies. With entry into the adult economic and political institutions which confer status beginning so early in life, it is not surprising that parents and other socializing agents would attempt to train children according to what they see as promoting their successful rise in society. In psychological terms, the early induction of children into adult institutions favors the parental perception of stimulus equivalence between the behavior of children and the behavior of adults in roles which could lead to social success or failure. From this perspective it is not at all fanciful to assume that a parent's concept of the ideal successful man would influence the manner in which he trained his children.

Having spelled out in detailed causal terms the process by which a status mobility system can affect child rearing sources of n Achievement, we must deal with McClelland's assertion that such a formulation assumes that parents know more about personality development than psychologists specializing in the subject. First of all, it is not asserted that parents are entirely conscious of what they are doing but only that their values as members of a wider society influence their dealings with their children, perhaps without their even being aware of this influence. Second, there is no reason to regard adaptive relationships between child rearing and social structure as implausible because they seem "too perfect," particularly if it is granted that there are processes of sociocultural evolution. The theory that the anatomies of plants and animals are well suited to their environments is not rejected on the grounds that this would involve an implausible structural anticipation of environments; rather, biologists search for the adaptive mechanisms by which such ecological relationships are attained. Similarly, in exploring personality and social structure, we must not close the door to the possibility that adaptations occur; on the contrary, we must direct our empirical search toward them. Third, the present formulation does not assume that all or even most parents produce children with the ideal personality characteristics, but only that the status mobility norms skew child-rearing practices in such a direction that a larger proportion of individuals exhibiting the characteristics will be found than in another population with different norms.

In this section we have presented the theoretical formulation linking the status mobility system in a society with personality traits such as *n* Achievement in its population. This formulation will assume concrete form in the following chapter, in which it is applied to three Nigerian societies. It remains to be explained here what grounds we have for expecting contemporary Nigerians to continue to be affected by their traditional, or nineteenth-century, status systems.

PSYCHO-CULTURAL LAG

If status mobility systems determine frequencies of achievement motivation in populations, a change in the nature of status mobility will cause a change in the relative frequency of achievement motivation. We must, however, expect that some time will elapse before the structural change has a discernible effect on personality. Few parents will be so sensitive to structural changes and adaptable in their social behavior as to change the emphases in child-rearing practices as soon as the changes in status mobility patterns have occurred, especially when changes in training are not immediately demanded by the new situation but only favored by them. Eventually the new type of child training will become normative, and parents will be under some pressure to conform, but the lack of an explicit ideology such as characterizes religious transformations may delay the diffusion of the innovations. It may be that a person has to grow up in the new value environment for his parental behavior to be seriously affected by it; if so, it would take about two generations for the structural changes to be manifested in the personality characteristics of the adult population.[35] Although the amount of time required is speculation, it seems highly likely that there will be a substantial — that is, easily perceptible — lag between the social change and the personality change it causes. Thus the level of *n* Achievement in a population may well reflect the status mobility system of a generation or more before.

In African societies there is even greater reason to assume that contemporary *n* Achievement levels reflect traditional social en-

---

[35] This is more time than is estimated by Alex Inkeles, in his major theoretical discussion of the subject, "Social Change and Social Character: The Role of Parental Mediation," in N. J. Smelser and W. J. Smelser (eds.) *Personality and Social Systems* (New York: John Wiley & Sons, 1963), pp. 357–66. In that article, however, Inkeles is dealing mainly with rapid and radical social change.

vironments. In most of the interior of tropical Africa, European administration began no more than three generations ago, and institutional changes seriously affecting status mobility occurred even more recently. Furthermore, such changes did not involve replacing traditional status mobility patterns, at least initially, but rather superimposing new ones on the old or setting them side by side with the traditional ones. For most of the population, living in rural areas or small towns, and separated by a huge cultural gulf from the relatively modernized cities, the more traditional status systems of their local areas retain a reality for them and an influence on them which is certainly equivalent to that of the new ones. Finally, Western innovations in requirements for status mobility have in every region been altered from their Western forms by combination with traditional forms (syncretism) and by reinterpretation along traditional lines. The total result is to dull the impact of institutional change on the values and personality characteristics of the masses. The recency and gradualism of large-scale institutional innovation in tropical Africa, together with the theoretically posited lag between structural change and personality modification, make it reasonable to assume that contemporary levels of n Achievement in African populations were shaped under the pressure of conditions before European influence was felt.

This idea draws empirical support from the South African work of S. G. Lee,[36] who concludes from a study of Zulu women's dreams:

Dream content . . . is derived almost exclusively from areas of social experience permitted by the culture *in the indigenous system of sanctions* of some 50 to 100 years ago. . . . This tends to confirm the Freudian hypothesis of the early introjection of the parents — the parents also, presumably, have relatively "time-lagged" superego values — and would mean that the super-ego content of the individual, at any rate in its more unconscious aspects, may have relatively little to do with contemporary values.[37] (Italics in original.)

In his earlier TAT study of educated South Africans he also uncovered evidence for this psychological time lag.[38]

On the basis of this time-lag theory, we venture in the following chapter to predict differential frequencies of n Achievement for three Nigerian ethnic groups from the differing characteristics of their pre-colonial status mobility systems.

    [36] S. G. Lee, "Social Influences in Zulu Dreaming," *The Journal of Social Psychology*, 47 (1958), pp. 265–83.
    [37] *Ibid.*, p. 270.
    [38] S. G. Lee, "A Preliminary Investigation of the Personality of the Educated African, by Means of a Projective Technique." Unpublished M.A. thesis, University of Natal, 1949.

3

STATUS MOBILITY IN NINETEENTH-CENTURY NIGERIA

When the three large ethnic groups of Nigeria came under British rule in the late nineteenth and early twentieth centuries, they differed drastically from one another in their systems of social stratification. In this chapter we attempt brief reconstructions of these systems, with particular reference to status mobility, on the basis of available ethnographic evidence. It must be stated at the outset that the pre-colonial Hausa, Ibo, and Yoruba had in common a number of relevant socioeconomic attributes which they shared with other West African societies. First of all, the three societies exhibited a relatively high degree of occupational differentiation on a base of subsistence agriculture. In each group, although men were tillers of the soil, there were many craft specialists as well as professional traders: for example, workers of metal, wood and leather, musicians, butchers, dyers and weavers, professional hunters, although not all were found in all three groups. Most of these occupational specialties were hereditary, being concentrated in particular lineages or compounds and passed on from father or uncle to son. Second, the Hausa, Ibo, and Yoruba all practiced slavery and engaged in active slave trading during the nineteenth century. Although slavery took different forms, slaves formed a significant segment of the population of each group. Third, in spite of slavery, none of these groups was a rigidly stratified society; in each there were some opportunities for freemen, and usually for slaves as well, to better themselves economically, socially, and politically. Status mobility was a characteristic of the Hausa, Ibo, and Yoruba societies in the nineteenth century, and some positions at or near the top of the locally recognized status hierarchy were often filled by men of obscure origins who had begun life with few resources besides their own skills and energies. Thus the variations in status systems among the three societies were not discrete differences in kind but major differences in degree and emphasis. The common characteristics formed a background against which we can contrast the divergence.

Several caveats and qualifications must be made concerning the reconstructions which follow. Wherever the term "traditional" is used, it is equivalent to "nineteenth-century" or "immediately pre-colonial." Both Hausa and Yoruba societies underwent great upheavals in the early nineteenth century, resulting in profound changes in status mobility patterns from the eighteenth-century base. It is clearly incorrect to assume that at the beginning of British administration any of the social structures was in its traditional form, if by "traditional" is implied an unaltered archaic residue of several centuries earlier. To dispel the possibility of confusion on this point, it must be understood that for the purpose of this study the late-nineteenth-century condition of these societies — on which we in any event have the most accurate ethnographic material and which is most likely to have an influence on contemporary behavior — is taken as the ethnographic present in preference to earlier periods.

Two other problems are posed for the comparison contained in this chapter. One is that the ethnographic materials on which it is based are uneven in their coverage of the points essential to the comparison. Numerous anthropologists have worked among and written about the Hausa, Ibo, and Yoruba; but few of them have been specifically interested in status mobility as such, and some have presented relevant data concerning topics on which others are silent. The comparison is necessarily blunted by this lack of comparable evidence. Furthermore, each of the ethnic groups is extraordinarily large for Africa and contains considerable internal variation in social stratification, not all of which is equally well described in the literature. Even where the internal variants are adequately documented, the predictive nature of this study has required that they be overlooked in favor of a generalized picture of each group's status system, and has meant making arbitrary decisions in order to capture the central tendencies of each system at the points of divergence from the other groups. The decisions were to concentrate on the characteristics of the central, dominant, or culturally purest subgroup for which most ethnographic evidence was available. The result is for each group a composite but selected description at a fairly abstract level of generalization, which does not hold true for a number of marginal or culturally mixed subgroups. Although subject to valid criticisms by experts on each of the three societies, the descriptions are able to serve adequately for the present comparative purposes because of the great magnitude of difference in central tendencies among the traditional status systems of the Hausa, Ibo, and Yoruba. It should be noted that errors of ethnographic characterization, whether they consist of overestimating the differences between groups or of other misinterpretation, increase the probability of failure in predicting the results of psychological testing. The greater the extent to which the following characterizations represent an excessive generalization of patterns drawn from a subgroup to the whole ethnic group, the less likely is a sample of individuals drawn from several varying subgroups to manifest the psychological dispositions hypothetically connected with the ethnographic description. The more the descriptions represent exaggerations of the actual differences between the three groups and underestimations of the internal diversity of each group (the "uniformitarian fallacy" of A. F. C. Wallace),[1] the less likely are the heterogeneous (with reference to subgroup) subjects to exhibit the ethnic group differences predicted on the basis of the ethnographic characterizations. Thus faultiness of ethnographic description in this chapter, although by no means desirable, leads to a more severe test of the hypothesis, rather than biases the results in favor of confirmation. In other words, if the differences among the three ethnic groups are so strong as to show themselves even when their prediction has been based on crude judgments that ignore sources of overlapping distributions between the groups, we can conclude that the differences are at least as potent as they seem to be.

THE HAUSA

The Hausa are a predominantly Islamic people, with a population of more than eight million in Nigeria alone, who inhabit northwestern Nigeria and adjacent areas of the Niger Republic. Although Islam was introduced among them more than five hundred years ago, its effect on the population was greatly intensified after 1804. At that time Fulani religious leaders in the town of Sokoto began a holy war that resulted in the rapid conquest of most of the Hausa territory and its reorganization as a series of semi-independent kingdoms under the orthodox Islamic and political leadership of the sultan of Sokoto. The most important kingdoms were Kano, Katsina, Sokoto, Zaria and Daura, each of which had its own capital city which was also a market center. At the time of British intervention in 1900, these kingdoms were autocratic monarchies

[1] Anthony F. C. Wallace, *Culture and Personality* (New York: Random House, 1962).

ruled by dynasties of Fulani origin who had intermarried with and adopted the language as well as many of the customs of the Hausa. The ethnic complexity of Hausa society was further increased in the nineteenth century by their massive capture and enslavement of the pagan peoples of Northern Nigeria. The Hausa language, Islamic religion, and slavery itself provided a framework for the rapid assimilation of large numbers of alien persons into the traditional Hausa culture as modified by the Fulani conquerors.

Nineteenth-century Hausa social structure is known exclusively from the publications of M. G. Smith,[2] who has written primarily on the Hausa of Zaria. Accordingly, our presentation is based on Zaria materials, but is followed by a discussion of the extent to which the characterization of that kingdom applies to the other Hausa states.

After the Fulani conquest in 1804, the Hausa political system (in Zaria) developed into what Smith calls a "short-term autocracy." Zaria was a vassal state in the Sokoto empire, and its king was appointed by the sultan of Sokoto from one of three dynastic lines among whom the kingship rotated. A new king had the power to discharge a large number of political officeholders and to appoint in their places his own followers, who were thus rewarded for their loyalty to him. Most offices carried with them fiefs — that is, territorial segments which the officeholder administered and in which he collected tax or tribute, keeping a part for himself and sending the rest to the king. The higher officials lived in the capital and had agents who managed their fiefs; there were local officials who replicated their rights and responsibilities at the village level. Although the king had advisers, there were no councils of any governmental importance; government was conducted through a vertical hierarchy of ranked officeholders. Commands flowed from the top down, and disobedience could be punished by removal from office (even the king could be, and was, deposed by the sultan of Sokoto); tax and tribute from fiefs and vassal chiefdoms flowed from the bottom up, with each officeholder deducting his part. In the frequent wars and slave raids, officeholders raised troops in their fiefs for the king and were handsomely rewarded with booty and captive slaves. So long as an officeholder retained the favor of the king through demonstrations of loyalty and obedience, he was allowed

[2] M. G. Smith, "The Hausa of Northern Nigeria," in *Peoples of Africa*, ed. J. L. Gibbs (New York: Holt, Rinehart & Winston, 1965); "Introduction," in *Baba of Karo: A Woman of the Muslim Hausa* by Mary F. Smith (London: Faber & Faber, 1954); *The Economy of Hausa Communities of Zaria* (London: H.M.S.O., 1955); "The Hausa System of Social Status," *Africa*, XXIX, (1959), pp. 239–52; *Government in Zazzau* (London: Oxford University Press, 1960).

to overtax and keep the surplus himself as well as to exceed his formal authority in a number of other ways. Thus the system had a despotic character, turning on relations of dependence and power between subordinates and their superiors. The rotation of the kingship among the dynastic lines, however, made the domination by any single group of state officials finite; when the king died, many of the officials were deposed as the new king brought his own followers into office.

The social status system in nineteenth-century Zaria was complex, but its basic outlines and its relationship with the political system are clear. At the top were those of Fulani ancestry (at least in their father's line), who were favored for office, especially those who were members of the dynastic lines and the hereditary nobility. At the bottom were slaves (about half the population of Zaria) and those of slave ancestry, who retained positions of subordination to their free masters and were eligible only for offices reserved for slaves. In the middle were the Hausa freemen, who were for the most part ranked according to hereditary occupation (mallams and wealthy traders at the top; cloth workers, silversmiths, commission agents, and farmers in the middle; butchers, tanners, eulogists, hunters, blacksmiths at the bottom; merchants varying according to wealth and other criteria) and who were eligible to all offices except those reserved for members of the royal lineages and those that were hereditary. Despite the largely ascriptive nature of this system of social placement, a man's fate was not entirely determined at birth. The principal means of rising socially, for those of both Fulani and Hausa ancestry, was by becoming the client or follower of someone of higher status (sometimes a kinsman, sometimes not) who would reward his loyal client with appointment to office if he himself was successful in obtaining an official position. In the early days of Fulani rule, many Hausa attained high office, but as the Fulani patrilineages expanded through numerous marriages with Hausa women, high-status Fulani competitors for office became numerous and began forcing out the Hausa. Nevertheless, most Fulani were not officeholders and were the political inferiors of those Hausa who were. High office led to personal enrichment, but many factors prevented the development of hard and fast social classes: the dynastic succession, which dismissed many officeholders when a new king came to power; the proliferation of Fulani lineages, which in Islamic inheritance distributed wealth equally among large numbers of heirs; and the general dependence of a man's fortunes on the favor and fortunes of his patron, which fluctuated. Thus falling socially was as common as rising; with each official who fell, so fell his numerous clients and his clients' clients, and so on.

Having sketched the outlines of the system, we must emphasize three points: political office was the most important means of acquiring wealth and social position, overshadowing other alternatives; clientage was the primary means of acquiring political office; clientage was widely practiced in the population and was an attribute of social organization at all levels. These points are amplified as follows in Smith's account:

Office provided its holders with opportunities for the accumulation of wealth, booty and slaves, and slaves were the main sources of farm labor. . . . An owner having sufficient slaves usually established his own settlement. This was called a *rinji* (slave-village or hamlet, plural, *rumada* . . .). The number and size of the *rumada* which a person or family controlled was evidence of the owner's wealth and power. Merchants and many other non-officials had slaves, but permission was necessary in order to build separate settlements for *rumada,* and this was generally given only to the nobility. In Zaria, the majority of the larger *rumada* were the principal forms of capital investment in Zaria, and thus political status was closely related to the distribution of wealth; conversely, the distribution of wealth was related to the distribution of political office.[3]

The king was at once the wealthiest and most powerful man in the kingdom.[4]

The extensive participation of Habe (non-Fulani Hausa) and Fulani in slave-raiding and war was achieved by mobilizing contingents from the fiefs; and military action offered such troops rewards in the form of booty, appointments and promotion. The frequency and success of these military adventures may have persuaded many people to support the system of government. Since political and administrative office provided the principal means of enrichment and social mobility together, and had clear military committments, the recruitment of officials for these expeditions presented no problem.[5]

These quotations serve to indicate that the greatest economic rewards in Hausa society went to the occupants of the highest governmental positions, from the king downward. It should be noted particularly that merchants in this highly developed mercantile economy were prevented from building slave villages, "the principal forms of capital investment," which were allowed to high officeholders. In addition to tax, tribute, and slave holding, the economic rewards of military action augmented the economic position of the official as compared with that of the nonofficial. Thus

[3] Smith, *Government in Zazzau,* p. 81.
[4] *Ibid.,* p. 93.
[5] *Ibid.,* p. 100.

in nineteenth-century Hausa society (in Zaria), political advancement led to wealth rather than the reverse. But what lead to political advancement?

Competition for office took a variety of forms. Of these clientage was perhaps the most important. Individuals might become clients of particular persons, such as officeholders eligible for promotion to the throne; or they might enter into a looser association with an important family or branch of a family; or one family or descent-line could be clients of another or of an office.[6]

Within the system of competing patrilineages, clientship served to bring Fulani and Habe (non-Fulani Hausa) into close political association thereby reducing the separateness and unity of these conquered groups. Solidary political relations of clientage were the usual bases of Habe appointments to office; and although offices allocated to Habe were generally subordinate to those filled by Fulani of noble lineage or royal descent, they provided their holders with opportunities for the accumulation of wealth, for upward social mobility, and for the exercise of power.[7]

Persons appointed to fief-holding office would normally have received some training in this political and administrative organization as subordinates or clients of senior officials. Dynastic personnel who were acquainted from youth with political competition and administration had less need for such training than others, and were occasionally given office at an early age. . . .[8]

The rule was for a new king to dismiss his predecessor's kin and supporters from important office, and to appoint people of his own. . . . Thus office circulated rapidly among an expanding population of competitors and this circulation of official position carried with it increased prospects of appointment for the numerous competing candidates. It thereby stimulated the development of clientage by the hopes of political competition, as the sole alternative to political impotence and loss of status.[9]

In distributing office among his clients, the king sought to elicit the widest possible support for his regime among the aristocratic Fulani and subject Hausa.[10]

In discussing the government of contemporary (1950) Zaria, Smith indicates that clientage is still the principal path to political advancement. Social status, he says, is based on occupation, income, kin-

---

[6] *Ibid.*, p. 83.
[7] *Ibid.*, p. 88.
[8] *Ibid.*, p. 100.
[9] *Ibid.*, p. 104.
[10] *Ibid.*, p. 121.

ship and marriage relations, age, slave or free ancestry, and conformity to Islamic prescriptions of wife seclusion and pilgrimage to Mecca, but:

An even more important type of relation which affects a person's status and prestige is clientage. . . . The client whose patron is successful in the quest for office, often has clients of his own, on whose behalf he seeks to exercise influence with his powerful patron. By fortunate relations of clientage, an individual may himself obtain political office, and thereby social mobility. Personal power corresponds with an individual's position in the structure of clientage relations which hold between and within the official and non-official sectors of the society as a political system. Although clientage is an exclusive relation, it may be changed or renewed as occasion warrants; and the client's capacity for independent political action and upward mobility alike may be a result of his ability to change patrons opportunely.[11]

From these statements we conclude that clientage — that is, being a loyal and obedient follower of a man's patron in his own struggle for office — was essential to the political advancement of all in the society except those who had hereditary claim to the very highest offices, and probably to them as well. The rapid circulation of incumbents in offices provided a strong incentive for ambitious clients, and the widespread distribution of clientage among subgroups whose allegiance was desired by the king, gave grounds for hope to those of humble birth. Successful clientage involved early training in habits of subordination and political intrigue and opportunistic choice of patrons. Once in office,

Its holder had two major committments: the first was loyalty to the king, and this allegiance was demonstrated by gifts and obedience; secondly, the official had to execute the king's instructions effectively and promptly, to collect the required tax, tribute, supplies or military detachments, and to discharge the various routine tasks already described. Throughout this system the great administrative sin was the sin of omission, the failure to execute promptly the order of one's immediate superior. Unless political disaffection was thereby expressed, actions beyond the strict authority of an individual's office were quite irrelevant. . . .[12]

Clearly, this system of status mobility placed a premium on loyalty, obedience, and sensitivity to the demands of those in authority over a man; excellent performance in an independent occupational role, self-instigated action towards goals that did not benefit the competitive chances of a man's patron, did not yield the man access to the major status rewards of the society and might conceivably damage his career. Furthermore, as suggested above, and shown

[11] *Ibid.*, 252–53.
[12] *Ibid.*, p. 106.

below, there were no significant alternatives to clientage and its authoritarian habits for a man of ambition.

Smith has described the ubiquity of clientage in Hausa social relationships: between top officials and their subordinate titleholders, between ordinary officeholders and their agents and community chiefs, between ordinary non-office-holding men, between wealthy merchants and their clients, and between women.[13] The single term *barantaka* refers to political, domestic, and commercial clientage, and denotes a relationship of unequal status in which the superior rewards the loyalty of his subordinate with office, title, wives, cash, or goods. The pervasiveness of clientage is well conveyed by Smith's remarks concerning its persistence in contemporary Zaria.

Differences of political maturity and minority are assumed and expressed in the structure of clientage relation. Among the Hausa a compound head is politically mature in the sense that he deals directly with his local ward or village chief, but normally he is also a client or dependent of some more powerful person, through whom he deals indirectly with the local chief of the latter's superiors. The compound head's patron is equally likely to be a client of some yet more powerful person through whom he seeks to deal with his rivals of comparable status, and with those officials whose activities bear on his immediate interests. At the top of this pyramid is the Emir. . . . "*L'etat, c'est moi*," is the constitutive principal of the emirate; and this being the case, its official hierarchic administrative structure is paralleled and combined with a hierarchy of unofficial clientage. . . . The competing leaders of groups of clients carry with them the political fortunes of their supporters, as well as those of their own kin. The client whose patron fails to secure office is at a disadvantage compared with him whose patron succeeds; and the more important the office secured by the patron, the higher the political status of the client. In such a system the commoner without a patron is not merely a deviant but also a rebel, since he admits of no personal allegiance; and such an individual occupies a disadvantageous position in this society. *The fact that some people nowadays avoid entering into clientage is frequently mentioned by Hausa and Fulani as an indication of overambition, disloyalty and of social disorganization through change. But these social isolates are few in number,* and are especially likely to emigrate.[14] (Italics ours.)

This indicates that clientage and its attendant patterns of subservience and obedience were inescapable aspects of social life in traditional and contemporary Zaria. Success in trading or acts of religious devotion might somewhat raise a man's prestige, but major social rewards beyond those to which he was born were achieveable only through clientage. Furthermore, refusal to enter into

---

[13] Smith, "Introduction," in *Baba of Karo*, pp. 31–33, and "The Hausa System of Social Status."

[14] Smith, *Government in Zazzau*, pp. 244–45.

clientage was socially punished in the sense that it put a man at a serious disadvantage compared to others and was also disapproved on moral grounds. This was a status system which strongly favored qualities of servility, respect for authority, allegiance to the powerful, and rejected qualities of independent achievement, self-reliant action, and initiative. The selective effect of this status mobility system was felt not only by the free Hausa and slaves, who were inferior by birth and could only hope to rise through affiliation with those of higher birth, but also by the high-born Fulani, whether commoners, noble, or royal, because their greater access to political office in the autocracy made their allegiances of great importance in the struggle for political power.

This description applies to Zaria, but what of the other Hausa kingdoms? Smith says that, in contrast to the administration of Zaria, the Fulani administrations of Daura, Katsina, Kano, and Sokoto were based on hereditary offices; favored clients of commoner birth could not occupy high office, although there were numerous offices reserved for slaves. Status mobility was altogether less common. In such situations the rewards of successful clientship were much less than in Zaria, but most evidence indicates that clientship and slavery were important forms of social relationship there too, and that independent achievement and self-reliant action were no more favored than in Zaria. In other words, a man of ambition with no hereditary claim to office had less chance of bettering his status dramatically through clientage in the other Hausa kingdoms, but that is not to say that he had a greater chance of bettering his status by any other means. On the basis of available evidence, then, we have no reason to conclude that the other Hausa kingdoms constituted more favorable environments for the man of self-reliant achievement than did the well-described Zaria kingdom.

THE IBO

The Ibo are a southeastern Nigerian people, with a population of more than seven million, who lacked political centralization, urban organization, and Islamic influence in the pre-colonial period. Dwelling mainly in the tropical rain forests, they practiced agriculture, trading, and crafts, and were importantly involved in the European slave trade from the seventeenth century to the middle of the nineteenth century. Actual contacts with Europeans in this period and until the twentieth century were confined to small numbers of mobile traders who visited or lived at the non-Ibo coastal areas; most Ibo operated in the hinterland as suppliers of slaves, other goods, and services to the coastal peoples. Although speaking related dialects and with many cultural similarities, the people whom we now call Ibo were traditionally more than two hundred politically independent territorial groups with their own local customs and social systems who conducted intermittent warfare against one another. Each autonomous group consisted of one or more villages or a community of dispersed settlement, organized along the lines of patrilineal descent groups. With few exceptions, internal decision making was performed not by a single leader but by councils of elders which, although some men were more influential than others, were highly responsive to the popular will. There were, varying from one area to another, age grades, title societies, individual title systems, or secret men's societies, which, together with the descent groups, served as organs for the differential allocation of social status and as channels for the flow of influence in the community.

Ibo social structure is known largely through the original work of C. K. Meek,[15] G. I. Jones,[16] M. M. Green,[17] and Simon and Phoebe Ottenberg,[18] although many other persons have written on various groups of Ibo. Few of the published works contain as much detail on social status as Smith's Hausa material, and those that do, deal with a single village or cluster of villages, which cannot be taken as representative of more than one local area. In consequence, we rely in this presentation primarily on summaries made by Ibo specialists whose acquaintance with the range of Ibo social structures is more intimate than our own. Despite the large number of regional variations and the lack of adequate detail, the basic outlines of the Ibo status system, and its striking contrasts with Hausa and Yoruba patterns, are so clear as to be easily presented in general form.

[15] C. K. Meek, *Law and Authority in a Nigerian Tribe* (London: Oxford University Press, 1937).

[16] G. I. Jones, "Ibo Land Tenure," *Africa*, XIX (1949), pp. 309–23; "Ibo Age Organization with Special Reference to the Cross River and Northeastern Ibo," *Journal of the Royal Anthropological Institute*, XCII (1962), pp. 191–211. Cf. also Daryll Forde and G. I. Jones, *The Ibo and Ibibio-Speaking Peoples of Southeastern Nigeria* (London: International African Institute, 1950).

[17] M. M. Green, *Ibo Village Affairs* (London: Sidgwick and Jackson, 1948).

[18] Simon Ottenberg, "Improvement Associations among the Afikpo Ibo," *Africa*, XXV (1955), pp. 1–28; "Double Descent in an Ibo Village-Group," *Proceedings of the Fifth International Congress of Anthropological and Ethnological Sciences* (1956), pp. 473–81; "Ibo Oracles and Intergroup Relations," *Southwestern Journal of Anthropology*, XIV (1958); "Ibo Receptivity to Change," *Continuity and Change in African Cultures*, ed. W. R. Bascom and M. J. Herskovits (Chicago: University of Chicago Press, 1958), pp. 130–43. Phoebe V. Ottenberg, "The Changing Economic Position of Women among the Afikpo Ibo," *Continuity and Change in African Cultures*. "The Afikpo Ibo of Eastern Nigeria," *Peoples of Africa*, ed. J. L. Gibbs.

The most characteristic feature of Ibo status systems, although not found everywhere, was the title society. This consisted in its most developed form of a series of ranked titles, the entry to which was contingent upon acceptance by existing titleholders, payment of a set entrance fee, and providing a feast for members of the society. Membership was open to anyone of free birth, but the fees and feasts effectively limited titleholding to those of some wealth. This was increasingly true as a man progressed to higher titles. Membership in the society entitled a man to share in the entrance fees paid by new members and to enjoy the prestige of titleholding. In many areas the title society also constituted a political oligarchy in the village or village-group, controlling the making of decisions even at public meetings at which all men had a right to speak and in which decisions were formally imposed by the heads of descent groups. The most important titles were not inherited, but fell vacant upon the death of a titleholder.

The title society was thus a means by which the wealth of a man could be translated into social and political status, ultimately the highest status which the local social system had to confer. In some areas the societies involved only a single title rather than a series of graded ranks; in others there were simply individual titles without a title society; in still others there were "secret societies." All shared the characteristic of providing individuals of exceptional wealth with exceptional authority and status. Furthermore, as Forde and Jones say, "Even where there was no title-taking a man of wealth could attain to considerable political power, apart from any authority derived from his place in a kinship system, because he could provide the gunpowder and firearms needed for raiding and protection, and could build up a considerable following." [19]

The evidence indicates that although the wealth necessary for acquiring high status could be inherited, it could also be accumulated through a man's own efforts; in either instance it needed to be accompanied by specific personal qualities. Ottenberg is quite definite on this point.

The Ibo are a highly individualistic people. While a man is dependent on his family, lineage, and residential grouping for support and backing, strong emphasis is placed on his ability to make his own way in the world. The son of a prominent politician has a head start over other men in the community, but he must validate this by his own abilities. While seniority in age is an asset in secular leadership, personal qualities are also important. A secular leader must be aggressive, skilled in oratory, and able to cite past history and precedent. A man gains prestige by accumulating the capital (formerly foodstuffs, now largely money) required to join title societies and perform other ceremonies. Much of the

[19] Daryll Forde and G. I. Jones, *op. cit.*, p. 20.

capital necessary for these activities is acquired through skill in farming and ability to acquire loans. Successful farming is a matter not merely of diligently using the proper agricultural techniques but often of a person's ability to obtain the use of the land resources of his friends, conjugal relatives, and his own unilineal groups. The ability to secure loans readily is a reflection of a person's prestige, the respect granted him, and the effectiveness of his social contacts. . . .

The possibilities of enhancing status and prestige are open to virtually all individuals except descendents of certain types of slaves and are not restricted to members of particular lineages, clans or other social units. Ibo society is thus, in a sense, an "open" society in which positions of prestige, authority and leadership are largely achieved.[20]

Farming was not the only means of acquiring wealth. As Ottenberg says, "A number of alternative paths lead to success and prestige. A successful man may be a wealthy farmer or trader, in some cases a fisherman, an influential priest, or an important secular leader. He may — though he need not — combine two or more of these social positions.[21] He points out that there are similar choices in religion (which is highly individualistic), the selection of associational groups, and the settlement of disputes, concluding: "Ibo culture thus provides alternatives which the individual must decide upon in terms of his own skill and knowledge. Their significance for the individual is that he rapidly develops experience in making decisions in which he must estimate his own position and opportunities for success."[22]

The over-all picture which emerges of the traditional Ibo status system is not only of an open system in which any freeman could attain high status but of one that placed a premium on occupational skill, enterprise, and initiative. The man more likely to rise socially is the one who was sufficiently self-motivated to work hard and cleverly marshal available resources in the cause of increasing his wealth. He must have had social skills, but these involved manipulating others to allow him use of their resources without becoming bound in subservience to them. His career was basically dependent on what he made of himself rather than (as among the Hausa) what he helped make of someone else. Higher social status was granted by the title societies and other agencies as subsequent recognition of a man's having already amassed wealth through occupational achievement and of his possessing capacities for leadership. The occupational performance was the primary locus of social evaluation, and performing well enough as a farmer, trader, or fisherman to obtain a title or provide firearms for followers required

[20] Simon Ottenberg, "Ibo Receptivity to Change," pp. 136–37.
[21] *Ibid.*, p. 138.
[22] *Ibid.*

the continual application of his own efforts in the service of his individual goals. Thus the Ibo man who rose socially could correctly
think of himself as a self-made man whose status mobility was a
recognition of his own individual achievements.

The nineteenth-century Hausa and Ibo status systems differed
in the following ways: As a large, centralized, and highly differen-
tiated hierarchy of ranks, the Hausa status system entailed much
greater differences in wealth, power, and prestige between top and
bottom statuses than the Ibo system. Social position was much more
determined by hereditary criteria (for example, Fulani versus Hausa ancestry) among the Hausa than among the Ibo. Mobility of
social status was connected primarily with the competition for political office among the Hausa and with economic role performance
among the Ibo. Individual status mobility (upward) was primarily attainable among the Hausa through the success of a man's
high-status patron, whereas among the Ibo it was through the man's
own success. The personal qualities most rewarded by higher social status were obedience, loyalty, and submissiveness to superiors
among the Hausa, and dedication to occupational achievement
among the Ibo.

The question of which system offered greater incentives for status
mobility is not easily resolved. On the one hand, it could be argued that the incentives were greater among the Hausa, since the
top statuses among them carried much more relative wealth, power,
and prestige than their nearest Ibo counterparts and since the rotation of dynasties afforded opportunities of advancement for many
groups of patrons and clients. On the other hand, an equally cogent
argument is that the high statuses of the Ibo, although less richly
endowed with dramatic status-transforming qualities, constituted
greater incentives for mobility because they were more attainable
by the average man, being less hedged by restrictions of birth and
more numerous in each local area. It is a question of whether the
magnitude of the goal or the chance of attaining it is more important in determining its strength as an incentive.

One point which is entirely clear, however, is that the Hausa status system was politically oriented, whereas the Ibo one was occupationally oriented. Among the Hausa, political office led to
wealth; among the Ibo, the acquisition of wealth led to political
power. Thus status mobility was achieved in one instance through
demonstrating capability of playing a role in an authoritarian political system, and in the other instance through the demonstration
of economic skills of an entrepreneurial sort. The ideal successful
Hausa man seems to have been the officeholder who faithfully supported his superior and rewarded his followers; the Ibo ideal ap-

pears to have been the energetic and industrious farmer or trader who aggrandized himself personally through productive or distributive activity. By Ibo standards, the Hausa ideal was overdependent and confining to the individual; by Hausa standards, the Ibo ideal was dangerously selfish and anarchic. A Hausa man who conformed to the Ibo ideal might amass some wealth, but would be prevented by his excessively independent spirit from winning the favor of the officeholders who control access to the major social resources. An Ibo man who conformed to the Hausa ideal might gain some friends by his inoffensive manner, but would lose in the individualistic struggle for wealth. Each set of status mobility values favored a man with different personality characteristics, and although it is by no means inconceivable that one man could combine both or change himself according to what was required, we propose that the relative frequencies of certain personality characteristics varied systematically between the Hausa and Ibo. The Ibo system was a more favorable environment for the man with *n* Achievement and is therefore likely to have produced a higher incidence of it in the male population.

THE YORUBA

The Yoruba inhabit southwestern Nigeria and adjacent sections of Dahomey, with a population of about six million in Nigeria alone. They have an ancient tradition of kingship, going back perhaps a thousand years, and dominated a large part of the West African coastal region and its hinterlands, under the Oyo Empire, until early in the nineteenth century. At that point the northern part of the empire came under the sway of Fulani invaders from the north, and the rest of it, which had been weak and divisive for some time, disintegrated into a number of warring kingdoms. The wars and consequent migrations and resettlements continued intermittently until British domination in 1890.

A Yoruba kingdom consisted of an urban center, in which the political, economic, and social affairs of the kingdom as well as a large part of its population were centralized, and some satellite towns whose rulers paid fealty to the king. Despite considerable variations in political structure from one kingdom to another, it can be generally said of these Yoruba states that their rulers were divine kings whose prestige and ritual status far exceeded their political power, and that one or more councils of state, consisting of hereditary chiefs and representatives of major territorial and associational groups in the town, were the main decision-making organs. Unlike the active Hausa kings, Yoruba monarchs were restricted by their divinity to their palaces, from which they rarely ventured. Although a Hausa king could be deposed only by his overlord, the sultan of Sokoto, Yoruba kings could be (and were) deposed and ordered to commit suicide by their councils, which selected the successor. Yoruba monarchy was far from autocratic, being rather lightly superimposed on a social structure which contained strong and independent groupings organized on the basis of lineage, territory, and associational (that is, age, religious, occupational) ties. For the most part these groupings selected their own leaders, who acted as a check on the central authority of the king and as a means for the development of a popular consensus on issues before decision making. Thus the Yoruba political system, despite its hierarchical form, was not an authoritarian one in which commands flowed from the king down the ranks of obedient officeholders; instead, power was dispersed among partly self-governing segments, with relatively little concentration at the center.

There are many excellent publications on Yoruba social organization by P. C. Lloyd, William Schwab, W. R. Bascom, and a number of others,[23] but the status system has not been described and analyzed as such. Like many other aspects of Yoruba society, the allocation of social status was complicated by the occurrence of many variations and alternatives and by an often misleading deviation of social reality from outward appearance. Concerning the disparity between appearance and reality, for example, the hereditary principle seems to have been strongly emphasized in Yoruba leadership, but on closer inspection it is revealed that from a large pool of possible heirs to a chieftaincy title a man would be selected who was wealthier, had demonstrated greater leadership capacity, and so on. There is no single principle of recruitment into high social positions that would adequately represent the complexity of nineteenth-century Yoruba society.

[23] P. C. Lloyd, "The Yoruba of Nigeria," *Peoples of Africa*, ed. J. L. Gibbs; "The Yoruba Lineage," *Africa*, XXV (1955), pp. 235–251; "The Traditional Political System of the Yoruba," *Southwestern Journal of Anthropology*, X (1954), pp. 366–84; "Sacred Kingship and Government among the Yoruba," *Africa*, XXX (1960), pp. 221–37; *Yoruba Land Law* (London: Oxford University Press, 1962). W. R. Bascom, "The Principle of Seniority in the Social Structure of the Yoruba," *American Anthropologist*, XLIV (1942), pp. 44–46; "Urbanization among the Yoruba," *American Journal of Sociology*, LX (1955), pp. 446–54; W. B. Schwab, "Kinship and Lineage Among the Yoruba," *Africa*, XXV (1955), pp. 352–74. Cf. also S. O. Biobaku, *The Egba and Their Neighbors 1842–1872* (London: Oxford University Press, 1957); Daryll Forde, *The Yoruba-Speaking Peoples of Western Nigeria* (London: International African Institute, 1950); J. F. A. Ajayi and Robert Smith, *Yoruba Warfare in the Nineteenth Century* (Ibadan, Nigeria: Cambridge University Press, 1964).

At the most general level, we can distinguish the following ascriptive statuses: members of the several royal lineages, who could inherit the throne; members of non-royal lineages in which chieftaincy titles were invested and inherited; commoners whose lineages had no hereditary claims to title; slaves. Among the commoners there were also hereditary craft occupations of varying status, but these were not as strictly ranked as among the Hausa. Birth into one of the four ascriptive status groups was only roughly correlated with ultimate social status, because institutions existed by which an individual could rise very high despite his birth. For example, in several Yoruba kingdoms there was the Ogboni society, sometimes called a secret society, sometimes a religious cult. It was in effect a kind of title association; although any adult male could join it, its higher ranks were open only to those who could pay the expensive fees. Its highest officers constituted a politically influential council in the central government, in some places the most important council surrounding the king. This, then, was a way of translating wealth, which might be amassed through occupational activity, into political power and status, in a manner resembling that of the Ibo title societies. On the other hand, however, there was the royal court, in which an individual could rise simply by gaining favor with the king. The king's favorite slaves and eunuchs were raised by him to positions of great importance and affluence, far exceeding most titled men in status. This status mobility pattern resembles Hausa clientage. Thus the Yoruba status system contained within it drastically different legitimate means of rising socially.

A critical difference between the Yoruba and Hausa systems is that the Yoruba kings and their officials did not have the control over the wealth of the society which characterized the Hausa governing elite. Chieftaincy did not involve fief holding, and did not thereby give access to vast sources of wealth. Even the king himself, although his court was lavishly provided for, was not permitted to enrich himself personally or his heirs through the permanent acquisition of property. Yoruba political officeholders, having much less control over their subjects than their Hausa counterparts, were in no position to exploit the kingdom's resources for their own benefit. There were, then, in trade especially, means outside and independent of the political system by which a man might make himself as wealthy as or wealthier than many chiefs of note. Furthermore, the Ogboni society and the appointment of wealthy men to council membership and even chieftaincy titles provided political recognition for men whose rise had been based on occupational achievement rather than political activity.

The anarchic state of nineteenth-century Yorubaland and the large-scale slave-trading activities provided unusual opportunities for entrepreneurial activity of a kind that was not possible in the more tightly centralized Hausa system. A dissident member of the royal family would raise a band of followers, migrate to a different place to found a separate town or join one of the new military centers such as Ibadan, and engage in slave-raiding and other military activities as well as establish a civil settlement. The loyal warriors of such a prince would be rewarded with land, slaves, booty, and even newly devised hereditary titles. This kind of pioneering and military adventurism occurred so frequently that it must have constituted a major outlet for the energies of the more individualistic Yoruba men throughout the mid-nineteenth century, and could have provided a substantial incentive for the development of achievement strivings. It should be noted, however, that it took the form of an authoritarian military organization with a patron-client relationship operating within it, so that the independence and self-reliance were likely to be limited to the founder of the new settlement, and he was likely to be of high birth. Moreover, such new settlements replicated the hereditary structure of the kingdoms from which they sprang. As in other Yoruba social behavior patterns, their pioneering too represented an amalgam of hereditary privileges and restrictions with opportunities for individual achievement.

On the basis of available evidence, we surmise that the status mobility system of the nineteenth-century Yoruba constituted an environment rewarding to both the independent occupational achievement of the Ibo ideal and the loyal clientage of the Hausa ideal. It is clear that there were many more status mobility opportunities for the independent man of occupational skill and industry who could not endure subservience than were afforded in Hausa society. It is equally clear that there were more hereditary restrictions, particularly on reaching the highest status positions, and more scope for success through sycophancy, than existed in Ibo society. The only possible conclusion is that Yoruba society was intermediate between Ibo and Hausa as an environment favorable to the development of n Achievement.

PREDICTED DIFFERENCES IN PERSONALITY

The foregoing analyses of the nineteenth-century status mobility systems of the Hausa, Ibo, and Yoruba can be summarized briefly as follows:

Hereditary restrictions on status mobility were greatest among the Hausa, but the rewards of wealth and power were also greatest in the centralized feudal autocracy that prevailed. The mobility system was politically oriented, and a man could rise only through clientage — that is, a relation of loyal and obedient support to a high-born person who was or might become a powerful officeholder in the authoritarian political system. Social incentives thus favored the subservient follower who could perform well in the political system over the independent entrepreneur or occupational achiever.

Hereditary restrictions were few among the Ibo; in the small-scale local status systems that prevailed, there were many opportunities for the average man to rise to the top. The Ibo status mobility system was occupationally oriented — that is, rising was dependent on individual achievement in pecuniary activity, with the resultant wealth being used to purchase social prestige and political influence in a ranked title society. Social incentives favored enterprise, diligence, and independent effort on a man's own behalf.

Yoruba society provided alternative paths of status mobility through occupational achievement in trading which could be politically recognized, as well as through political clientage in the royal court and in military adventures. It thus combined the Ibo and Hausa systems. Hereditary restrictions were, however, much greater than among the Ibo, and opportunities for mobility generally, and mobility through occupational performance specifically, were much greater than among the Hausa. Social incentives favored both the authoritarian political virtues of subservience and obedience (but less so than the Hausa) and the occupational virtues of enterprise and independent effort (but less so than the Ibo). If we assume that incentives provided by a status mobility system for some personality characteristics affect the actual distribution of such characteristics in the population for several generations, as specified in chapter 2, then we are led to predict that in comparable groups of Hausa, Ibo, and Yoruba males, the Ibo will contain the largest proportion of individuals with n Achievement, the Yoruba the next highest, and the Hausa the least. In the following chapters we shall test this prediction.

4

NIGERIAN SCHOOLBOYS:
SUBJECTS OF THE STUDY

In this chapter we describe the design of a study to test objectively the empirical validity of the hypothesis that differences in the incidence of n Achievement between ethnic groups correspond to differences in their traditional status mobility systems. In chapter 3 we demonstrated that the Hausa, Ibo, and Yoruba had status mobility patterns in the nineteenth century which differed in ways that should theoretically affect the relative frequencies of n Achievement in their populations. On the assumption of psychocultural lag — that is, a lapse of several generations between the onset of alterations in the status mobility system and consequent alterations in the frequencies of personality characteristics — and in the knowledge that social change for the Nigerian masses has been gradual rather than sharply discontinuous,[1] we decided to use youths drawn from the three ethnic groups as the subjects of the study. Since the interior of Nigeria came under British control between 1890 and 1920, a young person in 1961–62 would almost certainly have

[1] The persistence of Hausa clientage to 1950 was documented in chapter iii, above. Lloyd says of the Yoruba: "Technological and social changes are taking place in West African society at a faster rate than the world has ever known. . . . Yet these changes seem to be occurring among the Yoruba in such a way as to preserve much of the traditional social structure of the people. Yoruba society is still a peasant society. . . . The Yoruba town offers few opportunities to wealthy or educated strangers to achieve high prestige or political power; hence the desire of each man to retire to his hometown, where he is probably eligible for a chieftaincy title and will, at least, be a highly respected elder of his own large descent group." (P. C. Lloyd, "The Yoruba of Nigeria," *Peoples of Africa*, ed. J. L. Gibbs [New York: Holt, Rinehart & Winston, 1965], p. 577). P. Ottenberg emphasizes the persistence of old values for the Ibo of Afikpo and says: "Though virtually defunct by 1960, title-taking was still a going system in the 1950's." (Phoebe Ottenberg, "The Afikpo Ibo of Eastern Nigeria," *Peoples of Africa*, ed. J. L. Gibbs (New York: Holt, Rinehart & Winston, 1965), p. 17.)

four grandparents who were raised under traditional conditions — people from Lagos (a British colony since 1861) being the only exceptions — and many would have parents who were adults before the Western impact was felt. According to our theory, such individuals should manifest personality characteristics not substantially different from those of their forefathers.

THE SELECTION PLAN

Proceeding on this basis, we sought samples of Hausa, Ibo, and Yoruba youth for comparative study. Several practical considerations dictated the use of male secondary school students. The data had to be collected in the midst of ethnographic field work among the Yoruba of Ibadan; thus time in the Hausa and Ibo areas was drastically limited. The use of subjects other than students would have necessitated the translation of large quantities of verbal material into English from three African languages. We thought it unwise, in such a frankly exploratory venture, to devote to translation the considerable resources that would have been required. These considerations immediately ruled out the drawing of representative samples from the three ethnic populations; instead, we have tried to use internal checks and knowledge of contemporary Nigeria to detect any relevant bias in the groups of subjects that were ultimately drawn.

The plan we ultimately formulated was to select comparable groups of Hausa, Ibo, and Yoruba students from the top grades of the leading non-Catholic men's secondary grammar schools located in the cities (Zaria for the Hausa, Onitsha for the Ibo, Ibadan for the Yoruba) which are the main educational centers of the regions in which the three groups are situated. Students were to be taken from the top grades (fifth and sixth forms, the latter being roughly equivalent to junior college in the United States) of the leading grammar (academic) schools so that they would be able to produce verbal responses in English without extreme difficulty. Roman Catholic schools were ruled out because their greater emphasis on religious and moral instruction and their use of clerical personnel in teaching were considered a possible influence on values concerning authority, which were being investigated in a separate questionnaire instrument (which eventually proved to be unreliable and is not included in this report). Anglican schools, although conducted under Church auspices, are more neutral in this respect. Schools situated in the original homelands of the ethnic groups were selected in preference to those elsewhere (for example, Lagos), so that the subjects could be presumed to have been raised within the cultural milieu of their ethnic background rather than uprooted from it.

Deviations from this plan were made on several grounds: First of all, we wanted to include sufficient numbers of students with Western-educated parents and those without, to allow comparisons to be made; among both Ibo and Yoruba it was necessary to draw subjects from schools other than the ones with the best academic reputations in order to obtain enough students with uneducated parents. Second, we wanted to have not less than fifty subjects from each of the three ethnic groups; among the Hausa this required going outside the regular academic grammar schools. In each school all students in the grade selected were tested; those not belonging to one of the three ethnic groups were eliminated in the subsequent analysis of the data. A boy was classified as belonging to one of three groups if both his parents came from communities in the homeland of that group and if he reported that they spoke its language at home. Others were eliminated from the analysis. In the Zaria data collection it was found that a substantial number of Northern Yoruba boys happened to be included in the classes selected; these were retained as a separate group in the analysis of dreams reported in chapter 5.

THE SCHOOLS

Hausa subjects were drawn from three schools. The first was Government College, Zaria, the leading government grammar school in Northern Nigeria, in which the entire fifth and sixth (upper and lower) forms were tested. Second was the Provincial Secondary School, which serves all Zaria province, in which the fifth form was tested, there being no sixth form at the school. Although the total number of students from these two schools was sufficient, the number of Hausa students was not, owing primarily to the large number of Northern Yoruba and other non-Hausa students in the classes at Government College. There were four other possible schools in Zaria: an Anglican school, an agricultural college, the Nigerian College of Arts, Science, and Technology (now Sir Ahmadu Bello University of the North), and the Institute of Administration. The Anglican school was ruled out on the grounds that use of its students would allow the small, deviant group of Hausa-Fulani who are Christians to form too large a proportion of our Hausa group. The agricultural college was ruled out on grounds of questions concerning the English fluency of its students, and the Nigerian College was not included because it reportedly contained few Hausa students. Thus the Hausa sample was amplified by students in the Executive Training Program at the Institute of Administration, young men who had completed secondary school and were being trained for administrative positions in government. Unfortunately, these men, most of whom served in the government, were older on the average than other subjects, and a larger proportion were married. But the difficulty of obtaining Hausa subjects made us decide to keep them in; they are nineteen of the sixty-five Hausa eventually tested and included in the analysis.

The Ibo subjects came from the fifth and sixth forms of Dennis Memorial Grammar School, the leading Anglican boys' grammar school in Eastern Nigeria, and the fifth form of New Bethel College, which has no sixth form. The Government College (the leading government-operated academic school) was omitted from the Ibo group because it is situated not in Onitsha, where the testing was conducted, but in Umuahyia. Although the number of students tested at Dennis Memorial was sufficient in itself, New Bethel was chosen for further testing because as a smaller, commercially operated, independent school it was presumed to have a larger number of boys whose parents were less educated.

The Yoruba subjects came from the fifth and sixth forms of Ibadan Grammar School (the leading Anglican School) and Government College, Ibadan, and the fifth form of Ibadan Boys' High School. The last-mentioned was included for the same reason that New Bethel College was.

The question of whether the process by which students are selected and recruited into secondary schools could have affected the results of this study is a difficult one. It could be argued that since the entrance requirements for government colleges, universally regarded as the schools with the best students, are lower in the North than in the East or West, the Hausa students are likely to be of lower caliber than their Ibo and Yoruba counterparts. The use of substantial numbers of Ibo and Yoruba students from schools with less distinguished reputations should, however, have more than balanced that discrepancy. An argument on the other side is that since so few Hausa go to secondary school, those who do go are likely to be those highest in n Achievement, which would not be true among the southern Nigerians, who are more likely to go because of conformist motivation. If this were so, it would mean that the selection of subjects was biased against confirmation of the predictions. Any positive result obtained would have to be regarded as having been weakened by the selection procedure. We do not feel that the evidence is adequate for accepting the arguments on either side, but we believe ourselves justified in going ahead with the study on the grounds that there is no convincing evidence that the selection of subjects biased the results in favor of confirming the predictions.

THE STUDENT SUBJECTS

Altogether, 342 male secondary school students were tested and their responses analyzed; sixty-five were Hausa, thirty-three were Northern Yoruba, 106 were Southern Yoruba, and 138 were Ibo. The subjects ranged in age from fifteen through twenty-eight. Their mean age was nineteen; the median age was only a few months lower.

The Southern Yoruba, who were tested in Ibadan, are the group to whom the prediction about the Yoruba generally applies. The Northern Yoruba, who were included by chance in Zaria, are Yoruba who were conquered by the Fulani in the nineteenth century and who have been heavily influenced by Hausa-Fulani culture and sociopolitical structure. No separate examination was made of their status mobility system; it was arbitrarily assumed to be intermediate between Yoruba and Hausa, and the prediction of a correspondingly intermediate frequency of individuals with n Achievement was arbitrarily made.

The religious affiliation of the four groups of subjects is given in Table 1. Nearly all the Hausa students were Moslems; nearly all the Ibo, Christians; the Yoruba were divided, but predominantly Christian. We believe the Hausa and Ibo groups to be representative of the actual distribution of religious affiliation (except for pagans) in their respective ethnic populations, but the Yoruba group unquestionably contains a larger proportion of Christians than is true of the total Yoruba population, owing to the long-standing pattern of differential recruitment of Christians and Moslems into secondary schools among the Yoruba. Until recently, few Yoruba Moslems

TABLE 1

RELIGIOUS AFFILIATION OF SUBJECTS
BY ETHNIC GROUP

	CHRISTIAN	MOSLEM	OTHER OR NOT KNOWN	TOTAL
Ibo	137	0	1	138
Southern Yoruba	92	7	7	106
Northern Yoruba	22	11	0	33
Hausa	3	61	1	65
Totals	254	79	9	342

attended secondary school, partly because a large number of the schools at all levels were operated under Christian auspices. This situation is changing slowly, but Christians still far outnumber Moslems in completion of secondary schooling and in the ranks of the educated Yoruba generally. Hence we can say that our Yoruba groups are not unrepresentative in religious affiliation of the distribution of adherents found in the more educated segment of the

TABLE 2

SCHOOLING OF SUBJECTS' PARENTS
BY ETHNIC GROUP [a]

FATHER'S EDUCATION	IBO	S. YORUBA	N. YORUBA	HAUSA
(1) No school	26.0(36)	15.0(16)	75.8(25)	56.7(37)
(2) 1–5 years	23.9(33)	5.7(6)	21.2(7)	15.2(10)
(3) Standard six certificate	28.3(39)	15.0(16)	3.0(1)	16.7(11)
(4) Some secondary school	14.4(20)	25.5(26)	—	7.6(5)
(5) School certificate	.7(1)	28.3(30)	—	1.7(1)
(6) University	6.5(9)	11.3(12)	—	3.3(2)
Total	100 (138)	100 (106)	100 (33)	100 (66)

MOTHER'S EDUCATION	IBO	S. YORUBA	N. YORUBA	HAUSA
(1) No school	47.1(64)	33.0(35)	93.9(32)	92.4(61)
(2) 1–5 years	28.3(39)	13.3(14)	3.0(1)	4.5(3)
(3) Standard six certificate	20.3(28)	20.8(22)	—	3.0(2)
(4) Some secondary school	4.3(6)	25.5(27)	—	—
(5) School certificate	—	5.7(6)	—	—
(6) University	.7(1)	1.9(2)	—	—
Total	100 (138)	100 (106)	100 (33)	100 (66)

[a] Figures on the left are percentages; those in parentheses are the absolute numbers.

Yoruba population. Furthermore, the fact that Moslems form one-third of the Northern Yoruba group but less than 7 per cent of the Southern Yoruba is generally in line with the difference in proportion of Moslems in those two groups.

It should be stated that the Yoruba are the only people represented for whom affiliation with Islam or Christianity is a matter of individual choice. For historical reasons discussed by Coleman,[2] but which we shall not go into here, Christian missionary activity was largely prohibited among the Hausa, and the Ibo were almost completely unexposed to Islam. Thus it would not be correct to assume that for either group of subjects affiliation with the religion prevalent in their environment necessarily indicates a priori a rejection of

[2] James S. Coleman, *Nigeria: Background to Nationalism* (Berkeley and Los Angeles, 1958), pp. 91–112, 133–38.

other religions whose ideological premises and values are different. In other words, since most Hausa have no opportunity to be anything but Moslems, it is wrong to conclude that a Moslem Hausa has chosen Islam and rejected Christianity on the basis of the belief content of either religion; the same holds in reverse for the Ibo.

Table 2 shows the educational background of the subjects' parents. This is relevant in a study of n Achievement because it might be thought that students raised by Western-educated parents would have had greater exposure to the achievement values which are emphasized in Western culture. The distribution clearly shows the lead of the Southern Yoruba over all the other groups in frequency of highly educated parents. For example, the percentage of fathers with at least some secondary schooling — that is, in the top three educational categories — is as follows.

Southern Yoruba	64.1
Ibo	21.8
Hausa	12.1
Northern Yoruba	0.0

For mothers in the same categories, the same holds but even more extremely: whereas one-third of the Southern Yoruba subjects have mothers with some secondary education, only 5 per cent of the Ibo and none of the Hausa and Northern Yoruba have. In fact, most of the subjects from the latter two groups have mothers who have had no schooling at all, whereas only 33 per cent of the Yoruba and 46.3 per cent of the Ibo fall into this category.

Despite the obvious fact that the subjects as a whole have a higher proportion of educated parents than the total ethnic populations from which they are drawn, these relative frequencies of parental education roughly represent the relative educational progress of the ethnic groups as we know them (from accounts of the history of education in Nigeria).[3] The Yoruba of Western Nigeria — that is, the Southern Yoruba — were far ahead of any other ethnic group in Nigeria in schooling during the period in which the subjects' parents were growing up. The Ibo have been rapidly closing the gap, but their advances have been very recent. Western education in Northern Nigeria, where the Hausa and Northern Yoruba live, has been extremely rare for men and practically nonexistent for women. If we held the hypothesis that Western education of parents leads to n Achievement, we would predict that the greatest frequency of n Achievement would be found among the Southern Yoruba, followed by the Ibo, Hausa, and Northern Yoruba, in that order. The hypothesis proposed on the basis of the status mobility theory predicts a different order: Ibo, Southern Yoruba, Northern Yoruba, Hausa.

[3] *Ibid.*, pp. 113–40.

Evidence to help decide between these rival hypotheses is presented in chapter 5.

To summarize, the four groups of schoolboy subjects, although not strictly representative of their respective ethnic populations, do reflect the major religious and educational differences known to exist between their ethnic groups as a whole. The Hausa are predominantly Moslems of uneducated background, the Southern Yoruba, Christians of highly educated background; the Ibo, Christians divided on educational background; and the Northern Yoruba are divided between Christians and Moslems, but have uniformly uneducated parents.

5

ACHIEVEMENT MOTIVATION
IN DREAM REPORTS

To test the predictions concerning ethnic group differences in frequency of *n* Achievement, it was necessary to find a means of measuring this motive in the individual subjects. The usual means is by analysis of stories told in reaction to a series of pictures from the Thematic Apperception Test (TAT), but the pictures present a number of problems when used in comparative cross-cultural study: it is difficult to hold constant the meaning of a drawing depicting humans when it is used with subjects whose cultures vary considerably in their social customs, housing styles, and clothing. To take the last as an example, the Hausa, Ibo, and Yoruba differ so greatly in clothing styles and in the relative value of Western and traditional dress that any decision concerning the dress of figures depicted in a psychological test would be fraught with methodological perils. Similar problems arise concerning other verbal measures of *n* Achievement currently in use, and we did not regard the graphic measure as direct and convincing enough to adopt it.[1]

McClelland and his co-workers have applied the system they developed for scoring *n* Achievement in TAT stories to other kinds of verbal fantasy material, such as folktales and children's books.[2] Their assumption is that any imaginative production in narrative form can exhibit achievement content of a kind roughly similar to that of TAT stories, and for the same reason, as an expression of the creator's affective concern with achievement. Although the theory on which the TAT is based, that imaginative fantasies serve to express strong and often unconscious motives, stems originally from

[1] The comparative validity of verbal and graphic measures of *n* Achievement in a cross-national study is discussed in detail by David C. McClelland, *The Achieving Society* (Princeton: Van Nostrand, 1961), pp. 475–87.
[2] *Ibid.*

Freud's work on dreams, the n Achievement scoring system has never been applied to dreams. This may be because dreams are more difficult to influence and control experimentally than projective test responses, and because of the psychoanalytic emphasis on analyzing dreams for latent content, that is, infantile affects represented in heavily disguised form. In recent years, however, investigators such as Calvin S. Hall [3] and Dorothy Eggan [4] have demonstrated that the manifest content, that is, the actions and emotions explictly described in the dream narrative, can provide data on motives and other aspects of personality without "depth" interpretations of symbols. From her work on the Hopi Indians, Eggan concluded that recurrent dreams, "and the elaborations introduced into the recital of them, an integral part of the dreamer's associations with the dream, are all facets of a projective process in which the dreamer responds to his own mind's images of his culturally oriented world as it is, or as he wishes or fears it to be." [5] In a clinical study, Gordon [6] showed that TAT stories and dream reports collected from the same individuals are similar enough in both form and manifest content to permit a need-press system of analysis (from which n Achievement scoring derives) to be used on both.

Thus the available evidence suggested that manifest dream content resembled TAT stories as a medium for the expression of social motives like n Achievement. We decided to use dreams for the comparison of the three Nigerian groups, on the grounds that they would enable us to study the same aspects of personality as a TAT without the cultural contamination that the latter's pictures introduce.

The dreams were collected from groups of students in the classroom. The student was given two sheets of paper and asked to spend half an hour writing in English a description of the most recent nighttime dream he had had, and the next half hour writing a description of a dream he remembered having had more than once. These dream reports provided the raw data for the measurement of n Achievement. Although internal evidence indicates that most of the reports represent actual nighttime dreams as recalled by the subjects, some of them seem closer to daydreams. We made no distinction between

[3] Calvin S. Hall, *The Meaning of Dreams* (New York: Harper & Brothers, 1953).

[4] Dorothy Eggan, "The Manifest Content of Dreams: A Challenge to Social Science," *American Anthropologist*, LIV (1952), pp. 469–85; "Dream Analysis," in *Studying Personality Cross-Culturally*, ed. B. Kaplan (Evanston, Ill.; Row Peterson, 1961).

[5] Dorothy Eggan, "The Manifest Content of Dreams," p. 472.

[6] H. L. Gordon, "A Comparative Study of Dreams and Responses to the TAT: A Need-Press Analysis," *Journal of Personality*, XXII (1953–54), pp. 234–53.

the two types in our analysis. Our justification for retaining the day-dreams is similar to the following argument by Freud in *The Inter-pretation of Dreams:*

> Closer investigation of the characteristics of these daytime fantasies shows us how right it is that these formations should bear the same name as we give to the products of our thought during the night — the name, that is, of "dreams." They share a large number of their properties with nightdreams, and their investigation might, in fact, have served as the shortest and best approach to an understanding of night-dreams.
>
> Like dreams, they are wish-fulfillments; like dreams, they are based to a great extent on impressions of infantile experiences; like dreams, they benefit by a certain degree of relaxation of censorship.[7]

We did not, however, assume that all the reports constituted gen-uine descriptions of nightdreams or daydreams that had occurred, but only that they were fantasies produced in response to an am-biguous stimulus that did not dictate or bias the content of the story. In this sense, our procedure could be likened to the blank card of the TAT or to the Open Projective Test (OPT) of Forrest and Lee,[8] in which the subject is simply asked to produce a story that comes to his mind. The request for a dream probably allows a greater relaxation of the subject's censorship than these other techniques, since he has a lessened sense of personal responsibility for what are presented as the contents of his sleeping mind.

The students' dream reports were typed and disguised to elimi-nate ethnic identification, and were scored according to a slightly modified version of the McClelland-Atkinson scoring system for *n* Achievement in TAT stories. Neither of the scorers who worked on the reports had any knowledge of the hypotheses or the ethnic groups; the scoring was thus "blind." Other aspects of the procedure are presented in Appendix A.

Each dream report was classified as having achievement imagery (AI) present or absent. Achievement imagery was defined generally as reference to success in competition with some standard of excel-lence, and was intended to include concern with unique accomplish-ment and long-term involvement in attainment of an achievement goal. The criteria for classification are given in Appendix A.

Illustrative excerpts of dreams classified differently are presented below. The following two are Hausa dream reports; the first was classified as having achievement imagery present, the second one as having achievement imagery absent.

[7] From *The Interpretation of Dreams* by Sigmund Freud, Basic Books, Inc., Publishers, New York, 1955, p. 492.

[8] D. W. Forrest and S. G. Lee, "Mechanisms of Defense and Readiness in Perception and Recall," *Psychological Monographs*, 76 (1962), pp. 1–28.

It was on the last Saturday night with the full moon shining brightly in the sky. The night was warm, the air was still and I was full of joy.

As a refreshment, I went to an Indian film shown in the Rex Theatre that night. The film was called ANN. It was a long and interesting film that I did not come back to school until twelve midnight.

We saw in one scene of the film of how one man tamed a wild horse in an arena and won a prize. But the queen of the town, who was presenting the prizes, threw what the man won at him, showing that she was not satisfied with his success.

About the same thing happened to me that night. In my dream I found myself in an unknown city. A show was held in the arena of the city. The city was ruled by a beautiful young queen. I went to the arena myself and competed in some acrobatic events. I came first in walking on the hands, bull fighting, sword fighting, and shooting.

After the show, every winner was called to receive his prize. When I came for mine, the people shouted that they didn't know me, I was a stranger from somewhere unknown to them and so I can't get anything.

The queen, after hearing the complaints, asked me if I were a stranger and I answered yes. Hearing my answer, she asked two guards to take me to her palace for questioning. When the queen came to me in her place, she was alone and asked me my name and what I wanted in her city. I answered her that I wanted employment there and that my name was Mouktar. She for a while looked at me curiously and then gave me a nice cold drink from a silver cup, after which I fell asleep. When I woke up [in the dream] I found myself dressed in richly decorated clothes with a golden crown on my head. Moreover, my color changed from black to white to suit the color of the people there. There were soldiers around and on my right was the young queen. I was surprised how all this happened and I was about to ask the queen what all that was about when I was woken up. When I woke up I found myself wearing only my pajamas and my skin black as before.

Oh God! I had this dream about a year ago, I had it a month ago, I had it a week ago, I had it last two days, and I am sure that I shall have it tomorrow.

I usually dreamt that as I was sleeping in my compound beside my father or any place, I simply woke in the middle of the night. I then went out round the town with no weapon at all, and nobody was awake. When I was ransacking the town like a victorious general I suddenly became frightened and thought that something terrible must be following me and this thing, so I was told by my instinct, this thing wanted to harm me, to kill me. My head then began to beat more rapidly and at this time I just saw myself flying like an eagle. Flying not in an airplane; flying not with wings; but just flying. I continued to fly right into the sky. And the most wonderful thing about this dream is I could steer myself, I could control my speed, I could go as high as I wished or as low as I wished. But all these depended on my feeling towards that fearful thing which I felt was behind me. If I felt that it was near me, I just increased my speed. If, on the other hand, I saw that I could not go faster than that thing, then I would go higher and higher. When I felt tired and when I just wanted to rest I simply land on a building. Through these tactics I found that I escaped the fearful thing and so I returned home and slept again.

Here are two Ibo dream reports, with achievement imagery present in the first and absent in the second, according to our scoring.

From my childhood, I have been dreaming dreams but there is one particular dream which I dream often. Probably I may dream about it this night. The dream is in fact very simple but quite funny. Whenever I dream, I see myself as Albert Onyeonwuna, the Nigerian international footballer.

I saw myself as Albert Onyeonwuna being made the captain of Nigerian team in a football-soccer competition against Ghana. I dreamt that this match was played at Lagos stadium and that the Nigerian "Red Devils," with me as captain, defeated Ghana "Iron Gates" by two goals to nil. The match was played on a rainy day and the slippery ground added fun to what could be described as the most exciting match ever played in Nigeria.

Both teams started at a fast pace and with grim determination so that it was difficult to choose between the two. Suddenly I, as Onyeonwuna, came into the picture. I dashed for the ball and after beating Ghana's right fullback, sent in a fiery shot which left Ghana's goalkeeper sprawling on the ground. The people who were in the stadium jumped up from their seats in anxiety and started clapping their hands. From that time, there were anxious moments whenever I was in possession of the ball, for the people wanted me to score more goals. The applause had hardly died down when I received a short pass from our inside right winger, Emuke. I stopped the ball, and after beating Ghana's right halfback man, parcelled the ball with a short trip to our man in the centre forward. He was in the position to kick the ball when he was kicked down by the Ghana fullback man, and this attracted the referee for a penalty kick. I was the person who played the penalty kick and it was a clean goal. Thus I raised the goal tally for our team to two. We had only two minutes to go in the match and Ghana players, now tired and playing short of one man, were forced into a defensive game; thus we maintained the lead of two nil until the final whistle.

This is, in fact, the dream I dream most, and whenever I wake up the following morning, I become unhappy for I realize that I am not Onyeonwuna, but Alozie.

There is a certain dream which I cannot sleep for a month without dreaming of it since about two years now.

I have several times seen myself flying like birds in a dream. The first day I dreamt the dream, I was going to a certain place and I was attacked by a dangerous animal. To my surprise, I flew away and the animal could not harm me, as it did not know how to fly.

On one other day I was in a dream, there was something like war. An aeroplane was flying through our town and people were shouting that the enemies had come to throw bombs. I took a kind of gun and flew away. After I had gone up to a certain height, I shot the aeroplane down and there was no effect. Then we defeated our enemies.

In fact I have always seen myself flying like birds in a dream that I do not take notice of it again because it is almost constant. Whenever in my dream I have encountered any danger, I fly away like birds from the ground to the air.

The final two dream reports are Yoruba, with an achievement dream followed again by a report in which no achievement imagery was found.

Some elders in my town have often said that if somebody continues to dream the same dream over and over again, what he dreams of may likely happen. How far this is true still puzzles me. If, however, this generalization is true, I shall be happy.

I have always been dreaming that I had been awarded a scholarship to study chemical engineering in Western Germany. Very recently I dreamt that the same thing happened. Why I shall be happy if it can come true is that in Nigeria at present, there are few chemical engineers for the need of our industry which we want to develop. Therefore if I am given the scholarship to study there and after I had achieved my aim, I would come back to my country to serve and at the same time become an important personality in Nigeria. Each time I dreamt about it I do so in different ways. At times I might just find myself already being given some lectures or engineering. When I wake up again, I would simply find myself on my bed. Sometimes I might find that I was in a boat and suddenly, I would be told to come down because we had reached Western Germany.

In conclusion, all this made me believe that dreams are what we think of most in our mind and which we wish could happen per chance. Therefore we must not rely much on them, since they may or may not happen to us.

Just before I came in here this afternoon I lay quietly on bed with a novel in my hand; then my eyes began to grow heavy and were very soon closed — sleep had taken me away.

I found myself sitting down comfortably in the sitting-room of my girl friend's house. Unfortunately, she was not in, but her younger brother was with me in the parlor. We had a chat together for some time. After some time, I heard the voice of my friend downstairs and I became very excited. I quickly dashed down the stairs to welcome my friend — at this juncture the scenes of my dreams had shifted from my girl friend's house to my own house and my situation had also been shifted from that of guest to host.

Then I began to think of things to give her. I went in, opened the fridge [refrigerator] and brought out some bottles of Fanta [bottled orange drink]. By now the number of my guests had increased to five — some other girls had reached the sitting-room. How it happened only God knows. At any rate, I served my guests and all but my girl friend took their drinks. I implored her to take it but she refused; then I invited her to bedroom so that I could ask what the matter was. She entered with me, sat on my laps and I — you know — I, well, can't tell. I did not have any affairs but by the time she left my laps my dream had become a wet one.

Then food was ready for the two of us; we sat at the table and as I was just about to start upon the food, somebody woke me up and I had to come here straight for the questioning. Hence I was still so sleepy when I got here I thought my dream could continue until after I finished the food.

This is however a surprising dream because it is unusual of me to have wet dreams in the daytime. But there you are.

The level of motivation for each ethnic group was arrived at by a simple frequency count of the number of subjects in each group reporting at least one dream that was scored AI. The percentage and frequencies of such subjects in each of the ethnic groups are reported in Table 3. The order of the groups on percentage of AI dreamers is exactly the order predicted for frequency of n Achievement by the status mobility hypothesis; it is inconsistent with the prediction of the Western education hypothesis.

Each ethnic group was compared with each of the other groups, using χ^2. As shown in Table 3, the differences in percentage of AI dreamers between the Ibo and the Hausa and between the Southern

TABLE 3

PERCENTAGE OF AI DREAMERS
IN EACH ETHNIC GROUP

	PER CENT	N
Ibo	43 (60)	138
S. Yoruba	35 (37)	106
N. Yoruba	27 (9)	33
Hausa	17 (11)	65
Total	— —	342

ETHNIC GROUP PAIRS	χ^2 (1 df)	PROBABILITY
Ibo-Hausa	13.77	$p < .001$
Hausa-S. Yoruba	6.45	$p < .02$
Ibo-N. Yoruba	2.89	$p < .10$
Ibo-S. Yoruba	1.84	$p < .20$
Hausa-N. Yoruba	1.41	$p < .30$
S. Yoruba-N. Yoruba	.66	$p < .50$

Yoruba and the Hausa are statistically significant at the .02 level or less. The occurrence of the other differences by chance alone cannot be ruled out on the basis of this evidence.

These results are strikingly consistent with the hypothesis that the amount of social incentive provided by a status mobility system for individual achieving behavior is positively related to the frequency of *n* Achievement in the population. In chapter 3 it was pointed out that among the nineteenth-century status mobility systems in Nigeria, that of the Ibo was most conducive to individual achieving behavior, followed by the (Southern) Yoruba and Hausa, in that order. In chapter 4 we added the statement that the Northern Yoruba status mobility system could be regarded as less conducive than that of the Southern Yoruba but more so than that of the Hausa. The predictions from ethnographic evidence on social structure to individual personality data were supported in detail. It would however, be premature to accept the hypothesis without examining rival hypotheses that can also be tested by the data.

The hypothesis that Western education of parents is positively related to achievement motivation in children receives no support from the data in Table 3. As stated in chapter 4, the Southern Yoruba subjects have by far the greatest proportion of parents with Western schooling, followed by the Ibo, Hausa, and Northern Yoruba, in that order. We would predict, on the basis of Western education of parents, that the greatest difference in *n* Achievement should be between the Southern and Northern Yoruba; in fact, however, the two groups line up together in percentage of AI dreamers on the basis of ethnic similarity rather than being separated by the huge gulf of their difference in educational level. This is a striking indication that *n* Achievement is related to ethnic factors rather than to parental education.

It is possible to pursue further in these data the question of parental education and its effect on *n* Achievement. We can compare the incidence of AI among subjects with more and less educated parents, for the sample as a whole and for the Ibo and Southern Yoruba separately, as shown in Table 4. There those subjects with mothers who have five or fewer years of schooling are compared with those whose mothers have at least passed the standard six examination. Mother's education was taken as theoretically the most powerful influence on personality development, since the mother has the most contact with the child, especially in African societies, and since the mother's role in training for *n* Achievement has been so emphasized in the research literature. But Table 4 lends no support to the notion that mother's schooling is related to *n* Achievement in sons, the differences between educational groups being negligible in

TABLE 4

PERCENTAGE OF SONS REPORTING AI DREAMS WITH MOTHERS
IN ONE OF TWO EDUCATION CATEGORIES

MOTHER'S EDUCATION CATEGORY [a]	TOTAL SAMPLE PER CENT	N
1 – 2	33 (80)	243
3 – 6	37 (35)	94[b]
		337
Ibo		
1 – 2	45 (46)	102
3 – 6	43 (15)	35
S. Yoruba		
1 – 2	36 (17)	47
3 – 6	35 (20)	50

[a] Categories 1–2: mothers with no education through five years of education. Categories 3–6: mothers who have passed the Standard six exam and beyond.
[b] Five subjects were dropped for this analysis because there was insufficient information about the level of mother's education.

all three comparisons and actually in the reverse order, but not significantly, in two of them.

Another rival to the status mobility hypothesis is that religious differences account for the variations in n Achievement among the Nigerian subjects. According to such an hypothesis, Islam is a religion of obedience and respect for divine authority which discourages individualism and thereby n Achievement, whereas Protestant Christianity (characteristic of most of the Christian subjects) is a religion which encourages individualism and thereby n Achievement. This formulation would seem to be supported by the strong positive association between Christianity and percentage of AI dreamers for the sample as a whole ($\chi^2 = 12.52$; $< .001$). Religion, however, is almost completely confounded with ethnic group affiliation, since the two ethnic groups highest in percentage of AI dreamers — Ibo and Southern Yoruba — are overwhelmingly Christian, whereas the two ethnic groups lowest in AI are predominantly or overwhelmingly Moslem. The hypothesis can be adequately tested only if ethnicity and religious affiliation can be extricated, the ideal population for testing it being an ethnic group which contains sufficient numbers of Moslems and Christians for comparison. In these data, the only ethnic group which approaches this ideal is the Northern Yoruba. Table 5 presents the comparison of Moslem and Christian within the Northern Yoruba subjects on percentage of AI dreamers. There is no significant association between Christianity and frequency of AI manifest there. Hence we have no confirmation for the hypothesis that n Achievement is a function of religious affiliation as distinct from ethnic group membership.

Other hypotheses competing with the status mobility theory for explaining the pattern of results involve special drive-arousing circumstances differentially affecting the groups of boys reporting their dreams. The Hausa and Northern Yoruba students were tested in February, 1962; the Ibo in April of that year; and the Southern Yoruba in May. Those boys in the lower-sixth form had taken their school certificate examinations in December, 1961, and received notification of the results in March. The three-month wait involved a good deal of suspense, building up to a climax in March, just before the results were announced. When the Ibo lower-sixth students were tested in April, they had recently received their results, and it was felt that they might be preoccupied with examinations and thoughts of achievement and that their recall of dreams might have been affected by this preoccupation. We compared the Ibo lower-sixth boys with the Ibo fifth-form boys, who had been free of suspense over examinations. Sixty-four per cent (25/39) of lower-sixth boys gave AI dreams compared to 40.5 per cent (30/74) of fifth-form boys. This is a statistically significant difference ($\chi^2 = 6.76$, 1 df, $p < .01$). Thus the suspense over examination results seems to have increased the achievement imagery of the lower-sixth boys (assuming that other things were equal). This does not, however, ac-

TABLE 5

PERCENTAGE OF AI DREAMERS AMONG
THE NORTHERN YORUBA ACCORDING
TO RELIGIOUS AFFILIATION

	MOSLEM	CHRISTIAN	TOTALS
AI	27.2 (3)	27.2 (6)	9
Non-AI	72.8 (8)	72.8 (16)	24
Totals	100 (11)	100 (22)	33

count for the lead in frequency of AI which the Ibo showed over the other ethnic groups. Table 6 shows the comparison of the Ibo fifth form boys — those free of examination anxiety — with all the Hausa, Northern, and Southern Yoruba students combined. If the differences between the Ibo and the other ethnic groups were due entirely to the examination anxiety of the Ibo lower-sixth boys, there would be no significant difference between the Ibo fifth-form boys and all the others combined. The fact is, however, that the Ibo fifth-form boys did report a greater number of AI dreams, and the difference is significant at the .05 level. Thus we cannot accept the hypothesis that the ethnic group differences are due to the examination anxiety of one subgroup.

February, 1962, when the Hausa and Northern Yoruba boys were tested was the month of Ramadan, when Moslems fast from dawn to dark. Despite the heat and dryness in Zaria, they were not allowed to take a drink in the daytime, and the Moslem secondary school students seemed to adhere strictly to these prohibitions. There was the

TABLE 6

COMPARISON OF IBO FIFTH-FORM BOYS WITH BOYS
OF ALL GRADES AMONG HAUSA, SOUTHERN,
AND NORTHERN YORUBA

ETHNIC GROUP	PER CENT	N
Hausa, N. and S. Yoruba	28 (57)	204
Ibo, Fifth form	40.5 (30)	74
$\chi^2 =$	$- 4.00$	$p < .05$

possibility that this deprivation of food and water would arouse the hunger and thirst drives to the point that they would compete with other drives such as n Achievement and interfere with the occurrence of achievement dreams and /or their recall. O'Nell [9] has demonstrated that in the same set of dream reports, those of the Moslems show a significantly higher proportion of food and drink images than those of the Christians, for the sample as a whole. This is consistent with the drive competition theory, but it does not prove that the low frequency of AI among the Hausa was due to hunger and thirst arousal. The Northern Yoruba should have again proved a crucial example, being split between Moslems, who were presumably fasting at the time, and Christians, who were presumably not fasting. But, as Table 5 has shown, there is an identical frequency of AI for Moslems and Christians among the Northern Yoruba. Further research on the competition between physiological drives and n Achievement in dream recall is needed, but we are not yet ready to accept the hypothesis that the ethnic group differences reported here are due to hunger and thirst arousal. Our stand is based not merely on the insufficiency of proof but on the consistency of the dream results reported here with the ethnic group differences reported in subsequent parts of this study, in which drive competition could not have played a part.

In this chapter we have presented the frequencies of achievement

[9] Carl O'Nell, "A Cross-Cultural Study of Hunger and Thirst Motivation Manifested in Dreams," *Human Development*, VIII, (1965), pp. 181–193.

imagery in the dream reports of subjects drawn from the four Nigerian ethnic groups, and have found the relative frequencies to be in striking concordance with the predictions based on a theory linking n Achievement to status mobility systems. Four rival hypotheses, involving education of parents, religious affiliation, examination anxiety, and physiological drive competition, were examined in relation to the data but were not accepted as explanations of the results, largely because they were not supported by the available data. The status mobility hypothesis has thus far received stronger empirical support than any of these four competing hypotheses. This is not to say, however, that the status mobility hypothesis is the only plausible explanation of the ethnic group differences shown here; on the contrary, alternative explanations are offered in chapter 8, after presentation of the data on values, attitudes, and behavior in chapters 5 and 6.

6

ACHIEVEMENT AND OBEDIENCE
VALUES IN ESSAYS

In this chapter we present the findings of another aspect of the school study: the explicit values concerning achievement and obedience which the schoolboy subjects expressed when asked to write essays on success. The same subjects were assigned the task, in a classroom situation, of writing an essay in response to the question, "What is a successful man?", followed immediately by another essay on "How does a boy become a successful man?". For each essay they were given half an hour. Their responses were typed and masked and subjected to an objective line-by-line scoring for value motifs involving achievement and obedience-social-compliance (hereinafter referred to as OSC). In other words, measures were taken of the degree to which each boy saw achievement criteria and obedience and social compliance as leading to success. The scoring procedures, including scorer reliability, and the statistical methods employed in the analysis of the data are presented in Appendix B. The laboriousness of the content analysis scheme dictated a reduction of the number of subjects whose responses were analyzed; thus all sixty-five Hausa subjects were retained for this part of the study, and equivalent samples of sixty-five were randomly selected from both the Ibo and the (Southern) Yoruba.

Illustrations from the data are presented below, beginning with the complete essays written by a Yoruba student:

What Is a Successful Man?

A successful man is one who is able to move successfully with others in life. In this aspect, he will be almost certain of success in any project he undertakes. Among the qualities of a successful man are the ability to control people who are under him, making the best use of any opportunity so as to obtain maximum result, and to be able to move in almost any type of society.

Expanding upon these qualities, he is a man who can easily suit him-

62

self to any atmosphere to fit the temperament of the occasion. Once he can do this he is likely to win the favor of many people who will be willing to admit him into their society.

Another aspect is that he must be of good administrative ability so that he can control those people under him without necessarily incurring their displeasure. He should have organizing talent so that he can make the best out of any occasion. In short, he must be efficient and should be conscientious in his undertakings.

He must not display some bad attributes; the feeling of inferiority complex must be dispelled because he will feel himself out of a particular society of people who might help him. He should have some self-confidence in himself and self-control. His unselfish interest in others must show so that he can make many friends who will be ready to obey and help him.

He must abstain from doing evil or being unkind to others because he, as a successful man, will serve as a good example to others, and not a bad one.

Above all, the successful man must be a man of good will, considerate and kind, hard working and efficient, giving selfless service and devotions to others; he must have an organizing ability, a clean character and a feeling of good will to others.

How Does a Boy Become a Successful Man?

To be a successful man needs all the determination in a boy. His characters develop in him as he grows up and therefore his manners will be shaped by the external forces and internal forces working in him from his youth. As the quotation goes, "Behold, I lay in Zion for a foundation, a stone, a cornerstone, a precious cornerstone, a sure foundation, he that believeth shall not make haste."

In his youth, he must learn to move with the best boys, boys of courteous and unselfish characters. Boys who will not indulge in evils rampant with youths. An example is giving unkind gossips about others, pilfering and loafing and being rude to others above him. He should cultivate a pious character and this will help him to be respectful and unselfish.

He should not be timid of those above him, but approach them boldly if he has any question that may help him to ask from them. Thereby, he will not cultivate any inferiority complex. He must try to discourse fully with those who are already successful and try as much as possible to prevent walking with the debased and mannerless boys who may try to influence his manners in a fundamentally bad way. Also by walking with the high, his hopes will be with the high and not the low.

Women are the cankerhood of men. Boys who start flirting with girls will end up by achieving nothing. Their minds will go off their work and they will grow old to become philanderous and unable to eke out existence. So the boy who wants to be successful must not start being flirtatious.

In his work, he must be hard working and conscientious. He should learn to do everything to time, and present himself whenever occasion calls. He will then develop the habit of precision, efficiency and not become as lazy as a drone.

He must be respectful to his parents who are the people that can guide him successfully through life by their advice. He must not indulge in crude ways like thuggery or roguery.

He must learn to be interested genuinely in his friends and mates, and to accept mistakes when corrected, be conscientious, hard working, walk with the high and successful and abstain from evil. Then he will have laid as a foundation for his successful life, a precious cornerstone.

This set of essays in itself exemplifies the manifold meanings of "success" which appear in the responses and how greatly many of them deviate from the most widespread European and American concepts of success.

Here are examples of excerpts which are scored as manifesting achievement values.

A successful man should be able to take care of his business. A successful lawyer knows fully well that for him to retain his eminence he must be a responsible man, someone that can be trusted to argue a case to the best of his ability. He knows fully well that the more cases he wins, the more prominent he becomes and so he behaves himself in a respectable way. A successful business man that is a prosperous merchant knows fully well that he must master his business before he hopes for any more prosperity.

Closely allied to the sense of responsibility is dutifulness. A prosperous man must be hard working and a man who always applies himself to his work diligently. A successful teacher is one who always prepares his lessons before going into his classroom. He does not always depend on what he learnt at University, but reads to keep abreast with changing time. (Ibo)

Hardwork and success are twin-born. None can go without the other. A tailor cannot be successful unless he works hard; neither can a truck-pusher be successful unless he works hard. Indeed, even the politicians whom critical people look upon as not having merited their positions often discover that unless they campaign seriously and keep themselves always in the eyes of the populace, they lost the subsequent elections. Thus under any circumstances whatsoever, the successful man is primarily a hardworking man. He must have that quality of learning to work hard. (Ibo)

There comes a time when he [a boy] must choose what his later course in life must be. If he had been determined on one particular course since his junior days and had taken pains to work hard at the subjects concerned, he will find it easy to gain his heart's ambition. He must be undeterred and must work excellently.

A boy who wishes to be successful must have a cool head to deal with every fresh obstacle in his path. He must know he has one goal and one goal only and nothing must deter him from getting to that goal. (Yoruba)

Lastly but not least a successful man does not rest on his oars. If he is rich he continues to work for more money or else that which he already has will one day disappear. If he is successful academically, he continues to learn more, else his brain rusts in idleness. If he is a successful teacher, he continues to think out new methods by which his teaching will be more effective. Thus does one keep up his success. (Yoruba)

As soon as a boy is born, he is confronted by many obstacles which are very peculiar to man. These obstacles are quite inevitable. It is when they are overcome that a man can be counted as being successful. As we all know, every one of us has been given a very good talent by God . . .
It is said that a man must undergo through many difficult things before he can come to the top. An old man once told his son that he must do difficult things first. (Ibo)

He must work hard at his lessons. He must build up the habit of working hard from the very beginning of life's career. Besides working hard he must also play hard. If he does not play hard, he will not grow big and strong — ready to face any difficulties however great. (Hausa)

Here are examples of excerpts which were scored as manifesting OSC values.

However, a boy who is born among the people who always think deeply and identify good things from bad, always copies what he sees his elders are doing; thus when he grows to their age, he will adopt the same thing. (Hausa)

To be successful in life, a man must try to see that he does what is just, trustworthy, emulating, encouraging and undoubtful. In short, he must try to obey his seniors and parents in any sphere of life that he is adapted to. (Ibo)

In my own point of view, I can say that if a boy wants to become a successful man in life, he must always obey commands in every sphere of life that he thrives. Moreover, he must always try to take advices from his elders, parents and well wishers. In absence of this characters he is no where. (Ibo)

If a man . . . finds it difficult to train his children and wife, he is not yet a successful man. For a successful man should be able to train his children righteously and they should be well behaved, respectable and obedient to everybody who comes across them. In so doing people will actually agree that the man has not only been successful within himself but has been able to develop his children to be successful. (Yoruba)

At home, he must do all the parents order him to do if he can do this or follow the timetable at home, get the home training, do the morning piece of work given to him at home. I mean before he comes to school it will be part and parcel of his body and he just carry it on in school, this will help him in his school life and in future perhaps.

When he gets to the school he obeys the timetable definitely he will be reading constantly so, for he has got used to the timetable before, therefore the masters, the senior even the principal will like him. Once he has got the right hand of the principal who will recommend him for anything, I mean what is left he is successful at school, definitely that sort of boy will pass his examination.

The Principal will write a good report for him which he will take to the outside world. (Yoruba)

The following essay (in response to the second question) by a Hausa boy illustrates the inclusion of obedience in achievement concepts that was mentioned in chapter 1.

A boy is successful if satisfied that he has done his life's missions. So the first thing he should do, if he is to become a successful man, is to get for himself a target which will guide him in his walk through life. He is indeed successful if he manages to hit the target, and is very successful if he manages to do even better.

Whether he hits the target or not depends on the guide he gets at the initial stages of his life. It is almost certain that he will not get a good guide if he is rude to people. *So obedience is a very essential tool for the construction of a successful life.* (Italics ours.)

Having a good start in life is in itself not enough because anything may happen that may turn the table and if a boy has not got the right spirit he will just give up. It is most important therefore, if a boy is going to be successful in life, to cultivate the spirit of competition and the spirit of struggling under whatever circumstance.

After mustering these, then a boy has to work very hard in order to achieve the final goal. Hard work may be misdirected and thus in the end produce a discouraging result. But mental training helps to direct his hard work towards the right goal and produces a complete success in the end.

The criteria for scoring achievement value motifs included competition with a standard of excellence, self-imposed standards of excellence, self-imposed achievement goals, long-term involvement, instrumental activity, and obstacles, thus paralleling the motive scoring derived from the McClelland-Atkinson system. Numerical scores on achievement and OSC were obtained for each subject, and were equalized for length and converted to Z-scores. A multivariate analysis of variance was performed on all the value-motif scores, indicating that the mean differences are not due to differences in the degree of dispersion of scores between one group and another, and that the group means vary significantly from one another. Then t-tests were performed to assess the probability that each pair of differences between ethnic groups was due to chance.

The results for achievement value scores are presented in Table 7. Contrary to the prediction of an Ibo-Yoruba-Hausa order on achievement, the order shown is Yoruba-Hausa-Ibo. None of the ethnic group differences are statistically significant. In other words, there are only small group differences on the variable, so small that they might be due to chance, and the ones that do manifest themselves are not at all in the predicted direction. These data do not sup-

TABLE 7

ETHNIC GROUP MEANS, STANDARD DEVIATIONS,
AND DIFFERENCES ON Z-SCORES FOR
ACHIEVEMENT VALUES

		ACHIEVEMENT VALUES	
		MEAN	SD
Ibo	(N = 65)	− 0.10	.86
Yoruba	(N = 65)	0.09	1.00
Hausa	(N = 65)	− 0.00	1.12

ETHNIC GROUP PAIRS	t	PROBABILITY
Ibo-Hausa	.59	Not significant
Yoruba-Hausa	.50	Not significant
Yoruba-Ibo	1.19	Not significant

port the original status mobility hypothesis, and, further, they seem to us explicable only in terms of a testing artifact rather than a real group difference. In the scoring it was extremely difficult to eliminate mention of work and sacrifice toward success goals from being scored as achievement value motifs. It seems extremely likely, however, that many of the subjects mentioning work and sacrifice — in general terms — meant by them activity ordered by a superior and devoted to his ends rather than self-reliant occupational achievement. This possible ambiguity in meaning would serve to obliterate differences between subjects high in n Achievement and those oriented toward clientage. The language of achievement and its double-edged quality for Europeans and Africans, mentioned in chapter 1, seems to have affected the scoring according to a system devised exclusively for Western subjects. This rhetorical difference is of course more likely to show itself in generalized preachments such as these success essays than in dream reports, in which the subjects were unaware of being solicited for feelings about achievement. A related possible cause of the negative and theoretically uninterpretable results also concerns the explicit mention of success in the task provided the subject; this is discussed in connection with all the other findings in chapter 7.

A system was devised for scoring value motifs concerning OSC. The criteria included unquestioning obedience to those in positions of authority, undiscriminating emulation of respected persons, respect for authority as leading to success, and compliance to the desires of peers and subordinates. It was predicted, in line with the analysis in chapter 3, that the Hausa would be highest, the Yoruba

TABLE 8

ETHNIC GROUP MEANS, STANDARD DEVIATIONS,
AND DIFFERENCES ON Z-SCORES FOR
OBEDIENCE-SOCIAL-COMPLIANCE
VALUES

OBEDIENCE-SOCIAL-COMPLIANCE VALUES		
	MEAN	SD
Ibo (N = 65)	− 0.20	.83
Yoruba (N = 65)	− 0.09	.94
Hausa (N = 65)	0.29	1.06

ETHNIC GROUP PAIRS	t	Probability
Ibo-Hausa	2.88	p < .001
Yoruba-Hausa	2.23	p < .02
Ibo-Yoruba	.73	Not significant

next, and the Ibo lowest on this dimension. The results are presented in Table 8, where it can be seen that the predicted order occurred in the data and that, as in the dream data, the Ibo-Hausa and Yoruba-Hausa differences are statistically significant, whereas the Ibo-Yoruba difference is not. We believe this finding to support the notion that the clientage system, found strongest among the Hausa, promotes the holding of favorable values toward obedience and social compliance. The order of groups on this value dimension is the exact opposite of that on achievement imagery shown in chapter 5, indicating that values favoring obedience are not conducive to n Achievement. Thus, although the measure of achievement values seems to have been obscured by semantic ambiguities involved in soliciting a verbal response to explicit achievement-arousing stimuli, a measure of OSC taken from the same responses produces an array of data that support the predictions of the status mobility hypothesis about a dimension which appears both conceptually and empirically to be inversely related to n Achievement.

7

INDEPENDENT EVIDENCE ON ACHIEVEMENT
ATTITUDES AND BEHAVIOR

What is the impact on social behavior of the ethnic differences in students' motives and values shown in the two previous chapters? Although we have not conducted a separate investigation of this topic, we shall suggest here, by adducing systematic and anecdotal evidence on the social attitudes and behavior of the Hausa, Ibo, and Yoruba, that there are corresponding differences manifest in a variety of social situations which can be viewed as caused by (or co-symptoms of) the personality dispositions discussed earlier.

ACHIEVEMENT ATTITUDES IN A
PUBLIC OPINION SURVEY

In 1962, the same year as our school study, Dr. Lloyd A. Free, Director of the Institute for International Social Research, designed a nationwide public opinion survey of social attitudes in Nigeria which was carried out from September to November of that year by Market Research (Nigeria) Ltd.[1] The survey covered all Nigeria, with samples of the urban population and the rural population accessible by road being taken from each section. In all, twelve hundred interviews were conducted, with four hundred being arbitrarily assigned to each of the three regions, in order to avoid overinterviewing in the more populous North and underinterviewing in the more socially and politically active East and West. Ultimately 218 Fulani-Hausas, 431 Ibos, and 341 Yorubas were interviewed. Some open-

[1] The over-all results of this survey are published in Lloyd A. Free, *The Attitudes, Hopes, and Fears of Nigerians* (Princeton: Institute for International Social Research, 1964). The data presented here are based on figures given us by Dr. Free but which do not appear in the publication.

69

ended questions were asked concerning personal aspirations and aspirations for Nigeria; the responses are relevant to achievement.

One question asked in the survey was:

All of us want certain things out of life. When you think about what really matters in your life, what are your wishes and hopes for the future? In other words, if you imagine your future in the *best* possible light, what would your life look like then, if you are to be happy? [2]

The diverse responses were classified into a large number of categories, of which seventeen had frequencies greater than 5 per cent. The categories with the greatest frequencies are, according to Free, not dissimilar to the ones obtained through similar surveys in other countries — for example, improved or decent standard of living, welfare of children, good health for self and/or family. One of the

TABLE 9

PERCENTAGE OF EACH ETHNIC GROUP SAMPLE
MENTIONING SELF-IMPROVEMENT AS
LEADING PERSONAL ASPIRATION [a]

	PER CENT		N
Ibo	25	(108)	431
Yoruba	22	(75)	340
Fulani-Hausa	10	(22)	218
ETHNIC GROUP PAIRS	χ^2 (1df)		PROBABILITY
Ibo and Fulani-Hausa	20.24		$p < .001$
Yoruba and Fulani-Hausa	13.25		$p < .001$
Ibo-Yoruba	.944		not significant

[a] Data based on a survey conducted for the Institute for International Social Research, Princeton, New Jersey.

categories with an unusually high frequency in Nigeria, however, was "self-development or improvement," defined as "opportunity for independence of thought and action, for following through with own interests; further study." This is the type of response which might plausibly be expected of someone high in n Achievement. It was mentioned by 22 per cent of the total Nigerian sample.

The comparison of Fulani-Hausa, Ibo, and Yoruba is given in Table 9. The groups are ordered on this achievement-oriented personal aspiration as predicted by the status mobility hypothesis; the differences between both Ibo and Fulani-Hausa and (Southern) Yoruba and Fulani-Hausa being highly significant. This pattern of results corresponds in detail with that of the dream analysis (Table 3), and indicates a striking consistency between ethnic group differ-

[2] *Ibid.*, p. 24.

ences revealed in schoolboys' fantasy and those revealed in the public opinion survey responses of adults on dimensions related to *n* Achievement. These data lend support to the notion that groups producing achievement imagery in recalled dreams are more likely to have self-development as a leading personal aspiration.

Another question in the survey was:

Now what are your wishes and hopes for the future of our *country*? If you picture the future of Nigeria in the *best* possible light, how would things look, let us say, about ten years from now? [3]

The answers to this question were also classified into numerous categories, according to their emphasis, such as national unity, education, and so on. The largest cluster of responses (60 per cent) came under the general heading of "standard of living," which com-

TABLE 10

PERCENTAGE OF EACH ETHNIC GROUP SAMPLE MENTIONING
IMPROVED STANDARD OF LIVING THROUGH
TECHNOLOGICAL ADVANCE AS LEADING
NATIONAL ASPIRATION [a]

	PER CENT	N
Ibo	56 (241)	431
Yoruba	49 (167)	340
Fulani-Hausa	26 (57)	218

ETHNIC GROUP PAIRS	χ^2 (1 df)	PROBABILITY
Ibo and Fulani-Hausa	51.67	$p < .001$
Yoruba and Fulani-Hausa	29.17	$p < .001$
Ibo-Yoruba	3.53	$p < .10$ (not significant)

[a] Data based on a survey conducted for the Institute for International Social Research, Princeton, New Jersey.

bined two categories: "improved or decent standard of living or greater national prosperity in general" (18 per cent), and "improved standard of living or greater national prosperity through technological advances — increase in rate of mechanization, use of modern scientific advances; greater productivity in industry and agriculture; development of natural resources" (42 per cent). This last category, with its emphasis on technological advance, seemed to represent the very kind of concern which McClelland has attributed to the person high in *n* Achievement, whom he holds responsible for the economic growth of nations in the era of modern technology. Table 10 shows how the Fulani-Hausa, Ibo, and Yoruba compare in fre-

[3] *Ibid.*, p. 35.

quency of this achievement-oriented response. The order of ethnic groups is exactly the same as before and as predicted by the status mobility hypothesis. The differences between the Fulani-Hausa on one hand and Ibo and Yoruba on the other are again highly significant, whereas the Ibo-Yoruba difference, although in the usual direction, does not attain statistical significance.

The question arises as to why the group differences in achievement responses predicted by the status mobility hypothesis appear in these public opinion data as well as in the dream reports, but not in the value data presented in the previous chapter. Our explanation of this is that persons high in n Achievement are so preoccupied with it that they supply achievement themes and images to completely blank and ambiguous stimuli, like a request for recall of dreams or an open-ended question about the future; persons low on n Achievement are more likely to think of things unrelated to achievement when the stimulus is ambiguous, since they have no internal pressures operating to make them provide achievement themes. But when the stimulus itself provides external pressure in the direction of achievement response — by use of terms like "success" — then individuals low in n Achievement respond just as vigorously with the language of achievement, thus obliterating differences due to motivational level and substituting verbal differences of another order. Thus the value data on achievement in the previous chapter not only fused mention of hard work with mention of striving for excellence but also, by focusing the subject's attention on the notion of a "successful man," suppressed the difference between the individual who responds to internal cues concerning achievement and the one who responds only to external cues such as this task gave him. When the external achievement cues are not present, as in the dream reports and the public opinion survey, the predicted and more interpretable response pattern asserts itself.

Hence the ethnic groups having a higher frequency of persons with n Achievement also contain more persons concerned with their self-improvement and with the improvement of their nation through technological advance. We regard this congruence as illustrating the general effect of achievement motivation on personal aspirations and social attitudes related to economic growth. Individuals preoccupied with their own self-improvement and the technological progress of their country are, we believe, more likely to take advantage of modern institutional innovations when they are introduced and to favor and adjust to the changes associated with industrialization. They are probably more likely to prosper in a modernizing society, or at least in its most modern sectors. The significantly greater proportion of such individuals among the Ibo and Yoruba than among the Hausa is of great importance for economic development in their respective regions and for the contributions of these three groups to the national economic and political life of Nigeria. The small but consistent edge which the Ibo have over the Yoruba in achievement-oriented responses is probably also of greater importance for Nigeria's future than it would seem on the basis of the figures alone. We now turn to this Ibo-Yoruba differential in considering the outcomes of *n* Achievement in overt behavior.

CONTEMPORARY ACHIEVEMENT PATTERNS OF IBO AND YORUBA

In searching for patterns of achieving behavior in contemporary settings which might correspond to and be caused by the group differences in *n* Achievement, it makes no real sense to include the Hausa, since they have only begun to enter the modern arenas of competition in which such behavior is observable. The comparison must be limited to the Yoruba and Ibo, with particular attention to the acquisition of Western education and skills and successful entry into occupations requiring a high level of education, technical skill, or enterprise.

In the early 1920's, as Coleman [4] has shown, the highly educated Nigerian elite was almost entirely Yoruba, although so-called "native foreigners," mostly Sierra Leoneans, also played a prominent part. In 1921, for example, Yoruba formed 40.3 per cent of all those in urban areas of southern Nigeria who had received Western education, whereas the Ibo formed only 11 per cent. Of seventy-three non-Europeans in professional occupations, forty-seven were Yoruba and twenty-six were "native foreigners," there being no Ibo represented. Of the fifteen barristers, twelve were Yoruba and three were native foreigners. More than half the teachers and clerks were Yoruba, whereas only 12.7 percent were Ibo. The Yoruba advantage was due to much earlier contact with Christian missionaries, who had been active in their area since the mid-nineteenth century, and much greater proximity to the center of Western influence, Lagos, which was a Yoruba town.

From the early 1920's onward, in what Coleman has called "the Ibo awakening," the Ibo strove to catch up:

The Ibo embraced Western education with great enthusiasm and determination. Christian missions were welcomed, and were encouraged to set up schools in Iboland. Village improvement unions sponsored schol-

[4] James S. Coleman, *Nigeria: Background to Nationalism* (Berkeley and Los Angeles: University of California Press, 1958), p. 142.

arships, and Ibo students flocked to secondary schools in what is now the Western Region. By the late 1930's the Ibo were more heavily represented than any other tribe or nationality in Yaba Higher College and in most Nigerian secondary schools. Thenceforward the number of Ibos appointed to the African civil service and as clerks in business firms increased at a faster rate than that of any other group. By 1945 the gap between Yorubas and Ibos was virtually closed. Increasing numbers of Ibo barristers and doctors began to arrive from England. By 1952 the number of Ibos (115) enrolled at University College, Ibadan, was nearly equal to the number of Yorubas (118).[5]

One of the few measures of relative Ibo progress in professional occupations for which before and after figures are available is the number of physicians. In the early 1920's, there were twelve Nigerian physicians: eight Yoruba and four "native foreigners." In the early 1950's, there were 160 Nigerian physicians: seventy-six Yoruba, forty-nine Ibo, one Hausa-Fulani, and thirty-four others.[6] In three decades the Ibo had moved from zero to more than 30 per cent of the physicians in Nigeria. Their movement into other professions has been equally if not more dramatic, although no figures are available to demonstrate it. As of this writing, the Ibo seem to dominate a considerable part of Nigerian intellectual life: with top university administrators, the only three Nigerian novelists of international repute, university professors in fields ranging from botany and mathematics to history and political science, artists, and poets — all of whom are Ibo. This is a remarkable achievement for a people who had barely been introduced to Western education fifty years ago. The Ibo leadership in politics and government in Nigeria is perhaps their outstanding feat, and is documented in detail in the volumes by Coleman and Sklar.[7]

Apart from this success in becoming a major part of the modernized professional and governing elite of Nigeria, Ibo entrepreneurs, fanning out all over the country, have also enjoyed a substantial measure of success. Ibo have a reputation for being willing to take any sort of job, no matter how menial, when they first enter a town and then working their way up, living frugally and accumulating resources until they become wealthy. Some have made the most of traditional craft specialties like blacksmithing; others have found new specialties in rubber working, automobile repair, and other occupations involving new technical skills. To a town like Calabar, containing an old Westernized Efik population, the Ibo came during the 1930's and 1940's, found economic opportunities that the

[5] *Ibid.*, p. 333.
[6] *Ibid.*, p. 142.
[7] *Ibid.*; Richard Sklar, *Nigerian Political Parties* (Princeton: Princeton University Press, 1964).

Efik ignored, and soon became more powerful economically than the Efik, who were bitterly resentful.[8] The Ibo are clearly a group of great entrepreneurial activity whose drive for achievement and self-improvement has made them seek opportunities wherever they were and take advantage of any new situation that presented itself.

In Nigeria one frequently hears employers, teachers, administrators, and others who have had an opportunity to observe persons of several ethnic groups in comparable situations of task performance make invidious distinctions between these groups on characteristics related to *n* Achievement. One could dismiss such reports as stereotyped except that detailed independent accounts confirm each other, and in the absence of systematic objective investigation can be assumed to have a tentative validity. A typical testimony is this excerpt from an autobiographical memoir by Ezekiel Mphahlele, an African writer and *émigré* from South Africa, who came to Nigeria as a teacher in 1957:

During the first fifteen months I taught in a boys' grammar school. The complacency of the boys struck me forcibly, and I became progressively annoyed by it. . . . I was teaching mostly Yoruba boys in Lagos. The small number of Ibo boys in the school were a source of inspiration: critical, self-confident, challenging (even if sometimes obstructionist). Ibos are generally pushful; they have the guts to challenge authority. They seldom beg for favors, and I admire the man who does not beg for favors.[9]

It is unfortunate that we do not have comparable data of a systematic sort concerning the achievement-oriented behavior and occupational mobility of the Ibo and Yoruba in contemporary Nigeria. What evidence, anecdotal reports, and impressions we do have, however, indicate that the small but consistent difference in *n* Achievement between Ibo and Yoruba manifests itself in the educational and occupational achievement behavior of the two groups.

IDEOLOGICAL EXPRESSIONS OF IBO ACHIEVEMENT VALUES

Ibo achievement values are strongly expressed in their contemporary popular literature. Most of the inexpensive pamphlets printed in Nigeria for those of limited education are written and published

[8] Cf. Warren Morrill, "The Ibo in Twentieth Century Calabar," *Comparative Studies in Society and History*, V (1962–63), pp. 424–48.

[9] Ezekiel Mphahlele, "On the Long Road: From An African Autobiography," *Encounter*, XXII (1964), p. 41.

in English by Ibo in Onitsha and other towns of Eastern Nigeria.[10] One of the major themes of these pamphlets is how to get ahead in school, business, and employment. The titles are revealing: *How to Avoid Poverty, Money Hard to Get But Easy to Spend, Money Palaver, Man Works Hard for Money, Master of Money, Forget Me Not: Determination Is the Secret Key to Success, No Condition Is Permanent.* The last contains the following typical passage:

> When you are poor be an industrious man. Don't sit idle. You cannot win raffle when you do not sign it, it is when you sign it you will watch what will be the result. That is you cannot become rich when you do not work, it is when you work that you will begin to watch what your labour will produce. To be rich is very very hard but some people do not know. Some people think it totally a thing of chance. God cannot send you parcel of food or money from heaven. He can only bless and protect you.[11]

This is as explicit a statement of individualistic achievement values as can be found in the self-improvement literature of the United States or other countries in which the "Protestant ethic" was prevalent during the period of industrialization.

The influence of Ibo achievement striving on political ideology can be seen in most extreme form in the writings of Dr. Chike Obi, an Ibo mathematician and university lecturer from Onitsha who founded the Dynamic Party. In a pamphlet written originally in 1953, Obi propounded his ideology for an independent Nigeria.[12] Its primary goal is economic development for a nation viewed as being "about 300 years behind the advanced countries."[13] Obi advocated a "strategy of rapid advancement" involving "psychological mobilization" of the people through "total conscription."[14] This program, which he terms "Kemalism" after the Turkish model of modernization, requires military dictatorship because only this will "succeed in persuading the illiterate, ignorant, lazy, individualistic and undisciplined natives of Nigeria to make great physical and mental sacrifice . . . for the defence of their country and for the common good."[15] Obi views democracy as a "leisurely" form of government that can be afforded only by the Western countries, which already lead the world in science and technology.

[10] Cf. Nancy J. Schmidt, "Nigeria: Fiction for the Average Man," *Africa Report*, X, No. 8 (August, 1965), pp. 39–41.

[11] The Master of Life, *No Condition is Permanent*, (Onitsha, Industrial Printing Works, no date), p. 7.

[12] Chike Obi, *Our Struggle*, I (Yaba, Pacific Printers, 1962; second impression).

[13] *Ibid.*, p. 35.

[14] *Ibid.*, pp. 34–40.

[15] *Ibid.*, p. 24.

The doctrine that democracy and rapid economic development are incompatible does not seem consistent with our contention that achievement motivation is linked with anti-authoritarianism. It must be emphasized, however, that Obi is extremely hostile to *traditional* forms of Nigerian authoritarianism, which he sees as corrupt, backward, and lethargic. He views democratic forms introduced by the British as tolerating these very traditional authorities that keep Nigeria backward.

His antagonism to the persistence of traditional authority, and his estimate that traditionalism is strong, lead him to the conclusion that only a counter-acting authoritarianism will achieve modernization. Perceiving a necessary choice between achievement values and democratic values, Obi chooses the former.

As remote as Chike Obi's Kemalism was from the political views of Nigeria's national leaders in the first five years of independent nationhood, and as politically unsuccessful as his Dynamic Party was, he and his opinions were extremely popular among university students in the early 1960's. His outspoken criticism of corruption and incompetence in high places was widely admired among those who most favored rapid modernization, particularly young Ibo, even if it caused Obi to be imprisoned. The general strike of May, 1964, and the coup d'etat of January, 1966 (executed by young Ibo officers) must be seen as stemming from a kind of discontent and impatience to which Chike Obi gave voice in his writings and speeches even if he did not directly inspire it. It was the voice of achievement striving in the form of a political ideology taken more seriously by the Ibo than by other groups.

8

CONCLUSIONS

The most significant empirical findings reported in chapters 5, 6, and 7 are summarized in the following paragraphs.

In a study of Nigerian male secondary school students:

1. The frequency of achievement imagery in dream reports was greatest for the Ibo, followed by the Southern Yoruba, Northern Yoruba, and Hausa, in that order, as predicted by the status mobility hypothesis. The Ibo-Hausa and Southern Yoruba-Hausa differences are statistically significant. The order of the groups does not correspond to their ranking on frequency of educated parents. Differences between groups comprised on the basis of mothers' education are extremely small in the sample as a whole and in the Ibo and Southern Yoruba subsamples. Moslem-Christian differences are highly significant but almost entirely confounded with ethnic group membership. Among the Northern Yoruba, the only group with enough adherents of both religions, there is no difference in frequency between Moslems and Christians.

2. The frequency of obedience and social compliance value themes in essays on success written by the students was greatest for the Hausa, followed by the Southern Yoruba and Ibo, in that order. The Ibo-Hausa and Yoruba-Hausa differences are statistically significant.

In a nation-wide public opinion survey of Nigerian adults:

1. The proportion of persons mentioning self-development or improvement as a leading personal aspiration was greatest for the Ibo, followed by the Southern Yoruba and Fulani-Hausa, in that order. Ibo-Fulani-Hausa and Southern Yoruba-Fulani-Hausa differences were highly significant statistically.

2. The proportion of persons mentioning improvement of standard of living or national prosperity through technological advance as a leading aspiration for Nigeria was greatest for the Ibo, followed by the Southern Yoruba and Fulani-Hausa, in that order.

Ibo-Fulani-Hausa and Southern Yoruba-Fulani-Hausa differences
were highly significant statistically.

The Ibo have moved into higher education and professional
occupations, formerly dominated by the Yoruba, very rapidly and
in large numbers since 1920.

In the rest of this chapter we shall discuss these findings in relation to the three questions fundamental to psychological anthropology raised at the beginning of chapter 2. We shall attempt to draw
conclusions regarding the reality of the group differences revealed
in this study, their sociocultural causes or determinants, and their
consequences for the functioning of the Nigerian social and political
systems.

THE VALIDITY OF THE FINDINGS

Do the data presented above demonstrate a real psychological
difference between the populations studied? We raise this question
in its most extreme form because we believe it has been too often
overlooked by culture-personality investigators, who have not paid
enough attention to the validity of their measures of group differences. We have attempted to solve this problem by methods of cross-
validation — that is, by developing independent lines of evidence
that can be checked against one another in the way a historian checks
several documentary sources or an ethnographer checks informant's
accounts of the same events. Correspondence between facts independently arrived at makes it more likely that they represent an
objective reality and less likely that they are derived from a bias of
the instrument used to collect them. In this study, three methods of
cross-validation were used: checking different measures of the same
factor against one another, checking theoretically opposite factors
against one another, and comparing contradictory predictions concerning group differences on one factor.

Identical group differences in achievement motivation were found
in the analysis of the dream reports and in the public opinion data.
These two measures were alike in giving the individual a relatively
free opportunity to express his needs and wishes, but they were unlike in most other ways. The request for a dream report elicited an
elaborate personal fantasy in narrative form without asking directly
about personal desires; the survey questions asked directly about personal aspirations focused specifically on self and nation. The two different methods were employed by different administrators with
different samples of the ethnic groups under different conditions.
Thus their concordant results cannot be attributed to similarity in

method of approach, investigators, samples, or conditions of administration. Their independence and diversity make the identical group differences less likely to be due to errors of measurement in either.

The differences between the Hausa and the two other groups are supported by statistical tests in both bodies of evidence. The Ibo-Yoruba differences are so consistent in these data and in the information on achieving behavior that we are inclined to accept them as real (although of lesser magnitude) despite their consistent lack of statistical significance. The likelihood of such differences being due to chance is lessened by their replication in diverse sets of data.

The validity of the findings in this study can also be assessed by examining the relation of achievement motivation to a behavioral disposition that is theoretically opposed to it, authoritarianism. In theory, n Achievement is closely linked to self-reliance and individualism as personal attributes; hence, individuals and groups high on n Achievement should be low on submission to, and dependence on, authority. The more a man is disposed to yield to the commands of others, the less he is likely to set his own goals and strive to achieve them. It is logical, then, to predict that n Achievement should be inversely related to a measure of authoritarianism. The failure of our measure of achievement values in the schoolboys' essays prevented our running this correlation across individuals, but we did find the order of groups on obedience and social compliance values to be the reverse of their order on n Achievement. Furthermore, the same group differences were statistically significant on both variables. This predicted reversal on an independently defined and scored factor confirms the concept of n Achievement as antagonistic to authoritarianism as a personality dimension; it also indicates that our methods of assessing achievement motivation were measuring what they purported to measure, a dimension inconsistent with strong obedience values. This is another independent line of evidence supporting the likelihood that our group differences in n Achievement were not due to chance.

Finally, we can examine the validity of the findings by comparing the results predicted by the status mobility hypothesis, which involves real differences between ethnic groups, with those predicted by rival hypothesis, stating that apparent ethnic differences are masking underlying differences in acculturation, religion, examination anxiety, or temporary conditions of administration. These findings are presented in detail for the dream report data in chapter 5; they show that none of these factors accounts as adequately for the variations in achievement imagery as the assumption of genuine ethnic differences. The acculturation factor (as measured by parents' education) is most effectively examined by multiple comparisons:

across groups, across individuals for the sample as a whole, and within two subsamples. None of these comparisons yielded results predicted on that basis. The hypothesis that factors of examination anxiety or other temporary conditions of the schoolboys accounted for the group differences are made less likely by the convergent data of the public opinion survey, conducted with adult respondents in normal community settings. The religious factor cannot be ruled out, although subsample comparison among the Northern Yoruba did not support it. Thus the testing of hypotheses that cast doubt on the reality of ethnic group differences did not support the idea that non-ethnic factors could better account for the revealed differences in achievement motivation.

On the basis of the convergent support for the ethnic group differences from several independent and diversely varying bodies of evidence, and with the additional knowledge that data casting serious doubt on the ethnic nature of these differences have been sought and not found, we conclude that a strong likelihood has been established for the reality of the differences between Hausa, Ibo, and Yoruba reported above. This means that we find the evidence convincing enough to say that the differences found between the samples studied are probably characteristic of the populations and would manifest themselves in further studies using other samples and other instruments of measurement.

EXPLANATIONS OF THE GROUP DIFFERENCES

Assuming that the differences in n Achievement among Hausa, Ibo, and Yoruba are real, what caused them? Since we predicted these differences from the status mobility hypothesis, we tend to see proof of them as confirmation of that hypothesis. But do the findings constitute an adequate demonstration of the validity of that hypothesis, or are they susceptible to explanation on other theoretical grounds?

We are convinced that the results of the predictive study support the status mobility hypothesis but leave some relevant questions unanswered. The full theory assumes that a system of status mobility affects parental values (concerning the ideal successful man), which in turn affect their child-rearing practices, which in turn produce a certain level of n Achievement and other personality characteristics relevant to successful mobility. The findings presented in this study do not include data on parental values as such or on child-rearing practices, thus leaving open the question of whether these factors are necessary to explain the ethnic group differences. A more conclusive study would show correlations of *n* Achievement with child rearing, and parental values, both within and between groups. Furthermore, although we had hundreds of individual instances of *n* Achievement, there were only three instances of status mobility systems, and the Hausa, Ibo, and Yoruba differ in many other ways apart from status mobility: religion, population density, colonial history, and so forth. We cannot at present be certain that it is not one or more of these latter group differences that might account for the variation in achievement motivation. With a set of fifty diverse ethnic groups varying in both status mobility patterns and *n* Achievement scores, we could make comparisons that did not confound status mobility with other cultural or structural properties of groups. In such a sample it would be possible to examine the relation of religion and population density to *n* Achievement independently of status system, and to discover which of these group characteristics was the best predictor of *n* Achievement and what proportion of the variance in *n* Achievement each accounted for. Until this larger scale comparison is undertaken, our conclusions concerning the relation of status mobility to achievement motivation will remain tentative.

In the absence of a more conclusive study confirming the status mobility hypothesis, we can nevertheless compare that hypothesis with alternative explanations of the present findings. If we find these alternatives less plausible, we might retain our original hypothesis as the best explanation in light of the available facts; if we find one or more of them equal or superior in plausibility, we might reject or modify the status mobility hypothesis. Our examination of alternative explanations has as its aim not only the decision of which to accept but also a deepening insight into the problem of accounting for achievement differences between ethnic groups. The only determinant of these differences mentioned so far has been the degree of conduciveness of the traditional status mobility system to the self-made man. We now review three other possible determinants of *n* Achievement in groups: population pressure; withdrawal of group status respect; contemporary status mobility patterns. The discussion of each determinant separately is followed by a consideration of complex interactions of factors and of possible research designs for answering the empirical questions which have been raised.

Population pressure. The basic point here is that the Ibo homeland in Eastern Nigeria is one of the most densely populated regions in Africa, and overpopulation has been held responsible for Ibo activity in non-agricultural occupations. We are fortunate in having the case for this determinant stated by Horton as part of a theoretical argument concerning psychological explanation in anthropology and as applied knowledgeably to the Ibo.

Perhaps the most prevalent form of naiveté is the psychologist's readiness to accept certain obvious purposes and attitudes as ultimate, and to search at once for their causes. The social anthropologist, in many cases, would point out that these purposes and attitudes had "reasons." That is, he would show that they were not really ultimate, but on the contrary, were rationally justified by other purposes and attitudes lying beyond them.

The Ibo people of Eastern Nigeria have become renowned in recent years for the value they set on aggressive competition, the struggle for achievement, and the willingness to explore new avenues of power and status. A culture-and-personality theorist, whom I talked to about them, took this value as an obvious "ultimate," to be interpreted as the effects of certain causes — possibly in the realm of child training. As a social anthropologist, I was suspicious of this. I pointed to the fact that over much of Iboland there is acute land shortage, that anxious parents quite "reasonably" encourage their children to struggle for a school success that will fit them for some career other than farming, and that when the children grow up, their own "reason" tells them that their only hope of a comfortable existence lies in continuing the struggle in outside trade, or in jobs in government or the big commercial firms. To back up this interpretation, I pointed to the fact that in pockets of adequate land supply like Nike and Abakiliki, where everyone can still get along comfortably in a farming career, this syndrome of aggressive competition and readiness to exploit new avenues of advancement is not at all obvious.[1]

This position deserves serious consideration not only because the population pressure argument has a great deal of face validity for anyone acquainted with Nigeria but also because it presents a familiar and important challenge to psychological anthropology. Horton's hypothesis is that Ibo achievement behavior is a conscious, rational adaptation to an obviously difficult economic situation. The implication is that the Ibo response is that of any rational man in a coercive environment, and therefore needs no more complex psychological assumptions about the Ibo than that they can perceive their environment and are reasonable enough to want "a comfortable existence." We believe this rationalistic view does not help explain the most important aspects of the Ibo "syndrome of aggressive competitions."

The first important aspect of Ibo achievement behavior overlooked by Horton is that it was not the only "reasonable" course of action open to them. When a rural family is faced with a decline

[1] W. R. G. Horton, "The Boundaries of Explanation in Social Anthropology," *Man*, XLIII (1963), pp. 10–11.

in income such as that caused by overcrowding on the land, there is a choice between lowering standards of consumption and finding new sources of income. The former alternative, which involves becoming accustomed to increasing poverty, is in fact adopted by families in economically depressed areas all over the world. Such families operate on a principle of least effort in which the comfort of remaining in familiar surroundings and doing familiar things, even when faced with starvation, outweighs the future economic benefits that might be gained from drastically changing their way of life. So long as their impoverishment is gradual, they will put up with it, for it affords known and immediate gratifications that would be missing were they to seek new productive activities. Their behavior is by no means totally irrational; it is based on a short-run hedonistic calculus into which long-range considerations do not enter. To persons predisposed to adopt this course of action (or inaction), the Ibo willingness to uproot themselves and give up accustomed if reduced rewards, seems unreasonable and unnatural.

Another path available to the Ibo was that followed by the Hausa. The latter have not been reluctant to leave their land in search of nonagricultural income; Hausa traders are everywhere in West Africa. Their pattern of trade, however, is traditional, and no matter how long they stay in modern cities like Accra and Lagos, they remain conservative with regard to education, religion, and politics, and aloof from modern bureaucratic and industrial occupations. This does not seem to be an unreasonable adaptation, but it is very unlike that of the Ibo migrants to the same cities. There were, then, at least three possible courses of action open to the Ibo in response to their acute land shortage: to accept impoverishment at home, to extend traditional trading patterns while remaining as un-Westernized as possible, and to pursue Western-type economic activity with the changes in ways of life that were required for it. Other peoples have adopted the first two alternatives in response to economic adversity; although some Ibo undoubtedly did too, many chose the third course. The difference is not one of rationality but of energy and effort.

In simplest terms, the successful pursuit of a novel occupation involving a high degree of enterprise or education is not for a lazy man, no matter how hard pressed he is financially. To be as successful as so many Ibo have been they had to have adopted long-range goals of self-improvement, renounced immediate comfort and consumption in order to pursue these goals, applied themselves mentally and physically to this pursuit over a long period of time. Such efforts require extraordinary energy, of which many men are not possessed, no matter how poor they are initially; it is this energy factor that we call achievement drive or motivation.

Even if it be granted that population pressure caused the Ibo to seek employment in the cities, this would not explain why they strove to excel when they gained these opportunities. Every evidence we have indicates that Ibo, unlike many others, have not been content with "a comfortable existence"; they have restlessly worked toward the top in their new fields of endeavor. This crucial difference between simply making a living and persistent striving for long-range success is another point overlooked by Horton and unaccounted for in his rational adaptation hypothesis.

In our opinion, then, this hypothesis is unconvincing because it fails to explain those aspects of Ibo economic behavior that indicate a consistent pattern of success strivings above and beyond the need for subsistence. We do not reject as implausible a relationship between population pressure and economic achievement, but only Horton's account of the mediating pyschological factors involved. Achievement-oriented responses to overpopulation seem to be more common in Africa than in many other parts of the world, since a number of the apparently most enterprising African peoples, for example, the Kikuyu, are also among the most overcrowded in their rural homeland. This is a subject worthy of comparative research. If measures of n Achievement and achieving behavior could be obtained for a sample of African ethnic groups varying widely in population density or in capacity to subsist by agriculture, we could determine whether population pressure is related to achievement. Following Horton's suggestion of local differences in overcrowding and achieving behavior in Iboland, we could compare more and less crowded Ibo rural populations on n Achievement. Finally, we could carry such study one step further by comparing highly achieving Ibo individuals with their less enterprising fellows from the same areas on the amount of land to which they or their families had access. Until such investigations are carried out, we cannot be certain about the relationship of population pressure to economic achievement. Such a relationship would not be incompatible with our general formulation. It seems to us quite plausible that population pressure is translated into economic achievement in Africa through the child training practices of anxious parents which produce higher levels of n Achievement in their children. Investigation of the amount of time elasped between the onset of severe land shortage and the rise in achieving behavior would be crucial to the testing of this hypothesis.

This brings us to Horton's argument about "ultimates," by which he presumably means enduring behavioral dispositions which have a driving force of their own, as opposed to adjustable perceptions of the changing environment. Although mentioning Ibo encouragement of children's academic achievement, Horton clearly does not believe that this encouragement produces in the individual a disposition to achieve that is later applied to economic behavior; the economic achievement is seen as based independently on a perception made in adulthood concerning available occupational opportunities. This implies that the adult achieving behavior is a specific economic response to an economic challenge or incentive; there is no reason or pressure for Ibo to manifest achievement strivings outside the economic sphere. There is evidence, however, that Ibo manifest such strivings in a variety of non-pecuniary activities. Mrs. Ottenberg, discussing the values of the rural villages of Afikpo, mentions achievement in connection with athletic contests, a feature of traditional Ibo village life that has remained important.[2] The efforts and accomplishments of many individual Ibo in art, literature, science, and nationalist politics have been conspicuous and cannot be reduced to pecuniary motives. Their tendency to achieve seems as strong in athletic, cultural, and political activities as in business, civil service, and the professions. The generality of this disposition can be seen also in the data of this study, in which samples of their behavior ranging from dream reports to hopes for the future of Nigeria showed the Ibo ahead of other groups on achievement. This consistent performance suggests an internal drive that seizes the opportunity for expression in any type of situation rather than a specific adjustment to economic necessity. As Horton's hypothesis fails to account for the supra-rational energy involved in Ibo achieving behavior, so it cannot explain the generality of that behavior, particularly in nonpecuniary spheres of activity.

To return to our original consideration, does population pressure vary concomitantly with *n* Achievement in the three ethnic groups of our study? There can be no question that population pressure among the Ibo is more severe than in the other two groups. With rural densities ranging above one thousand per square mile,[3] the Ibo home country is one of the most overcrowded in Africa. The Southern Yoruba have an average density of three hundred to four hundred per square mile,[4] and their rural homeland has been one of the most prosperous agricultural areas in West Africa. Cocoa cultivation in particular has provided a high income yield from land, and there is arable land available that has not been farmed. The

[2] Phoebe Ottenberg, "The Afikpo Ibo of Eastern Nigeria," *Peoples of Africa,* ed. J. L. Gibbs (New York: Holt, Rinehart & Winston, 1965), p. 6.

[3] Cf. Simon Ottenberg, "Ibo Receptivity to Change," *Continuity and Change in African Cultures,* ed. W. R. Bascom and M. J. Herskovits (Chicago: University of Chicago Press, 1958), pp. 130–43.

[4] Galletti, Baldwin et. al. *Nigerian Cocoa Farmers* (London: Oxford University Press, 1956).

situation among the Hausa is not strictly comparable to that of the other two, since they inhabit a different vegetation zone with less rainfall; the densities vary greatly from one local area to another. It is clear, however, that the Hausa have not experienced the severe population pressure that the Ibo have. Thus the difference in n Achievement between the Ibo and Hausa might be accounted for in terms of population pressure, but the consistently significant differences between Yoruba and Hausa cannot be explained in this way. The Yoruba and Hausa are closer to one another in their ability to subsist adequately through agriculture, but the Yoruba are much closer to the Ibo in achievement motivation. The effect of rural population pressure on n Achievement cannot be ruled out, but does not account for the results obtained herein. It is to be hoped that the questions raised by the population hypothesis receive the systematic research attention they deserve.

Withdrawal of status respect. Hagen [5] has raised the question of why a "traditional society" or some group within it will suddenly abandon traditional ways and turn its "energies to the tasks of technological advance." His theoretical answer is that "the basic cause of such change is the perception on the part of the members of some social group that their purposes and values in life are not respected by groups in the society whom they respect and whose esteem they value." [6] The group so affected by "withdrawal of status respect" is first demoralized and then prompted to find alternative means of righting itself with the disparaging wider society. In so doing — a process which Hagen believes to involve changes in child rearing and personality development — the group assumes a role as technological and economic innovator, thus promoting economic growth in a hitherto stagnant society. Can this concept of withdrawal of status respect account for the differences in n Achievement among our three Nigerian groups? We must examine their history under colonial administration to find out. The Ibo could certainly be considered to have suffered a withdrawal of status respect during the early colonial period. Before British administration they constituted a relatively isolated cluster of societies, although they traded with coastal groups and some of their other neighbors. Once they came under British rule, however, various factors — their traditional entrepreneurial energies and/or population pressures — induced many of them to move to coastal towns like Lagos and Calabar and other centers of population. In those places they found peoples, like the Yoruba and Efik, who had had much more West-

[5] Everett E. Hagen, *On the Theory of Social Change* (Homewood, Ill.: Dorsey Press, 1962).
[6] *Ibid.*, p. 185.

ern contact and education and were firmly entrenched in the best civil service jobs and professional positions. These sophisticated peoples despised the Ibo not only as bush people lacking in Westernization but as savages whose traditional culture lacked cloth and clothing, urbanism, and political centralization, and allegedly involved cannibalism. Being regarded as naked savages from the forest with an inferior culture must have hurt many Ibos profoundly. Coleman has mentioned both the resentment and the ethnocentric Western scale of values which gave rise to the disparagement:

Educated Ibo leaders have been particularly resentful over the cliché that Africans have no culture and no history. . . . Many early European observers glorified the cultures, traditions, and histories of the Hausa states, and, to a lesser extent, of the Yoruba kingdoms, to which the Ibo, and other groups similarly placed, were invidiously contrasted.[7]

Out of their resentment at being despised as a backward people, and also at being discriminated against in jobs and housing in towns dominated by other ethnic groups, may have come the tremendous Ibo determination to get ahead, to be more modern than anyone else, to favor technological advance, and to succeed in every field individually and as a group.

It can be argued with equal cogency that the events since 1900 have afforded the Hausa maximal protection from the withdrawal of status respect which often accompanies colonialism. In the system of indirect rule they were allowed to retain their own rulers and continue the traditional life fostered by those rulers. Lord Lugard's agreement insulated them from Christian missionaries and Western education,[8] so that they never suffered the jolts to cultural self-esteem which are inflicted on a non-Western people by mission Christianity, by knowledge of the outside world, and by a new scale of educational values. In other words, they could continue to see as undiminished in splendor their traditional culture with its monarchy, orthodox Islam, orientation toward Mecca, and Koranic schooling. They did not suffer the invidious comparison with European culture or Europeanized Africans which southern Nigerians did. Furthermore, they maintained their autonomy until they were able to enter into a federation with the southern regions with themselves as the dominant leaders, having a majority of the voting population under their control. Hence, when the Hausa-Fulani political leaders came to Lagos, they came as the rulers of the Federation of Nigeria, without having to bow their heads to the Nigerians who had acquired

---

[7] James S. Coleman, *Nigeria: Background to Nationalism* (Berkeley and Los Angeles: University of California Press, 1958), p. 338.

[8] *Ibid.*, pp. 133–40.

European sophistication. Although the history of the Ibo indicates they were maximally exposed to disparagement in terms of the European scale of values introduced by colonialism, Hausa history indicates that they were maximally insulated from it.

The Yoruba were intermediate on withdrawal of status respect; although they were not insulated from the inevitable disparagement involved in intensive missionization and Western schooling, they received these blows to their cultural self-esteem so early, relative to the other groups, that they were able to view themselves as superior to the less Westernized peoples. Furthermore, although their traditional culture did not receive the respect paid by the British to Hausa culture, its monarchical tradition and associated cultural complexity protected the Yoruba from a low evaluation of their own group as contrasted with Europeans.

If, then, we view the three ethnic groups in terms of the hypothesis derived from Hagen that withdrawal of status respect leads to something like n Achievement, we can indeed find support for such a hypothesis. The Ibo, leading in n Achievement, certainly suffered the most complete group loss of respect during the colonial period; the Hausa, lowest on n Achievement, were most insulated from the conditions producing social disparagement in a colonial society; and the Yoruba, in a sense, had it both ways. On the basis of our Nigerian comparison, we cannot reject the theory which views achievement striving as a reaction to group disparagement, and we must admit it as a plausible explanation of our findings. The only fact it cannot explain is the greater achievement orientation of the precolonial Ibo as compared with the Hausa and Yoruba.

Contemporary status mobility patterns. A final alternative hypothesis arising in the course of analyzing the data is that the ethnic group differences in n Achievement are due to variation in the *contemporary* situations in status mobility in the three groups. Since the contemporary status mobility system of the group is a complex precipitate of the traditional system, its modification under colonial administration, and the present state of economic opportunities, this hypothesis is an eclectic one in which there is room for several of the factors hitherto considered.

The basic idea in this hypothesis is that the frequency of n Achievement in a group is determined primarily by the more or less accurate perception of the growing male child as to: the chances of his rising socially, and the behavior which leads to success in the status system. His perception is determined by the information concerning the state of the system which he receives from various individuals and institutions, including older members of the family, school teachers, religious instructors, books, and mass media. Let us assume that he forms a fairly stable image from these diverse sources of information by the time he is fourteen years old. If his image is that the chances of his rising socially are good and that individual competition with a standard of excellence is what leads to success, then he will manifest the achievement motive. If his image is that he has little chance of rising socially and that obedience and social compliance lead to what success is available, then he will not manifest the achievement motive. Intermediate examples will vary between these extremes, according to the amount of the perceived opportunities and the strength of the perception of achievement behavior as instrumental in success. Thus the frequency of n Achievement in a population will co-vary with the strength of the incentives for achievement behavior perceived by the men as being offered by the status mobility system during the years in which they were growing up. In this theory there is little time lapse between changes in status mobility system and changes in n Achievement, at least in the younger generation, and neither parental values nor child-training practices are involved as mediating variables — only the transmission of information to the child.

How does such a theory explain the findings of this study? Beginning with the Hausa, we can say, following Smith, that both the hereditary privilege of the Fulani and the institution of clientage have strongly survived into the present (at least as of 1950, when he did his study), and determine the magnitude and nature of opportunities in the contemporary Hausa status mobility system. This is, of course, because the colonial policies of indirect rule, prohibition on Christian missions, and slow development of Western education had enabled the traditional system to survive almost intact into the present. Thus a Hausa boy who was nineteen in 1962 would have grown up with an image of the possible in status mobility which was not drastically different from that of a boy growing up in 1865, the date for which Smith provides a picture of the traditional system. Our analysis of that latter system, then, holds good for the present, uncontaminated by notions of local democracy, the individual Christian conscience, and achievement of high status through successful education, and reinforced by Islamic injunctions of obedience as the highest virtue. The conclusion is that our sample of Hausa students, and the Fulani-Hausa adults surveyed in the national poll, had their level of achievement motivation formed by a status system which, now as in the past, does not offer strong incentives for independent achieving behavior.

Making the same assumption about the perceptual relationship between contemporary status mobility patterns and level of n Achievement, we have to consider rather different social factors in the Ibo case. Let us assume that the traditional Ibo system at very least predisposed Ibo children to be unusually sensitive to information about opportunities for alternative paths of rising socially and, specifically, opportunities for rising through occupational performance. The overpopulation and consequent decline in local agricultural opportunities forced adults to seek increasing amounts of information about outside opportunities in a variety of types of work, information which in the normal course of events was passed on to children. The flow of this type of information was vastly increased by the work of Christian missions and Western schools, which furthermore operated — along with the development of Western bureaucratic institutions in government and commerce — to create new institutional settings for the advancement of achievement-oriented persons through the acquisition of education and modern technical skills. The current generation of Ibo (including those whose behavior was sampled in 1962) reached maturity with a high level of n Achievement aroused and reinforced by the strong incentives for achieving behavior which they perceived by being exposed to an extraordinary amount of information concerning opportunities outside their local and traditional horizons. Thus the status mobility system which incites their achievement motivation is that of all modern Nigeria, not that of their local environment.

The Yoruba occupy the intermediate position, according to this theory, because, although they were exposed even earlier than the Ibo to a great deal of information about modern occupational opportunities and advancement through schooling (because of Christian missions, widespread Western education, and the introduction of Western bureaucratic institutions), the other side of the picture was balanced by local agricultural prosperity (primarily through cocoa farming) which reinforced not only the traditional occupation of farming but also many segments of the traditional sociopolitical status system. Since opportunities for wealth and status enhancement existed in agriculture, and land tenure was traditional, it was possible for ascriptive aspects of the traditional status system to be bolstered directly or indirectly through agriculture. A Yoruba youth would reach maturity with the perception that opportunities existed locally and in old-fashioned institutions as well as in the translocal world of modern achievement. Although he would perceive many incentives in the latter — hence his much greater level of n Achievement than that of his Hausa contemporaries — he would be more likely than his Ibo counterpart to be attracted to reliance on modified forms of local clientage, which have managed to survive in the contemporary Yoruba social structure.

This theory of contemporary status mobility and achievement

motivation does plausibly account for the ethnic differences in *n* Achievement which form the core of findings in the study. Its central difference from the theory of traditional status mobility presented in chapters 2 and 3 is that the latter involves parental values of individualism and specific training of the child in independence and achievement to develop the achievement motive, whereas the former assumes that a status mobility system can communicate its incentives to the child fairly directly and cognitively, without the familial manipulation of his motives. It is possible to devise research designs which would pit these theories against one another in contradictory predictions. The theory originally proposed predicts that, regardless of the contemporary system and its incentives, only those individuals who have been subjected to certain routines of independence and achievement training will manifest *n* Achievement; the other theory predicts that *n* Achievement will vary from one group to another concomitantly with the contemporary state of opportunities and incentives, independently of specific training routines in the individual life history. The next step is to conduct comparative studies of *n* Achievement with measures of child rearing and the perception of opportunities as part of the data collection procedures.

We believe that our discussion has illuminated the problem of finding determinants for the ethnic group differences in *n* Achievement, but it has not led us to reject as implausible all of the alternatives to our traditional status mobility hypothesis. More definite conclusions must await further research.

SOCIAL AND POLITICAL CONSEQUENCES OF THE GROUP DIFFERENCES

Whatever their origins, the motives, attitudes, and behaviors reported on here seem to have some clear implications for the directions of social change in Nigeria. This investigation indicates that associated with well-known regional variations in levels of economic development and Westernization in Nigeria are individual behavioral dispositions of a deep-seated nature which are probably resistant to change. If this is true, they will continue to influence Nigerian social life, at least in the foreseeable future.

The behavioral dispositions studied are not randomly or uniformly distributed among the three major ethnic groups of Nigeria; they vary significantly, and form a distinctive cluster. The cluster consists of achievement motivation, concern with self-improvement, non-authoritarian ideology (here measured through obedience and social compliance values), a favorable attitude toward technological innovation, and rapid advancement in Western education and the Western type of occupational hierarchy. The Ibo and, to a lesser extent, the Yoruba are high on all of these dimensions; the Hausa are low. This should not be interpreted as a simple absence in the Hausa instance, but rather as an attachment to an authoritarian ideology probably strongly reinforced by continued training in Islamic orthodoxy, a personal fatalism (probably also reinforced by the Hausa version of Islamic doctrine), and a conservatism in educational and economic affairs.

One effect of this clustering of dispositions is that those individuals most prepared to occupy the positions of professional, technical, and bureaucratic leadership in the newly formed Nigerian nation are persons favoring the modern advance symbolized by technological innovation and antagonistic to traditional authoritarian government and doctrines of passive obedience. As the southern Nigerians (Ibo and Yoruba) race forward in preparing themselves for these positions, the inevitable conflicts between them and the Hausa leaders of the North (who dominated the federation politically until 1966) have assumed an ideological as well as a sectional flavor. It is not simply Hausa versus the ethnic groups of southern Nigeria, but conservatism versus modernism, authoritarian versus democratic ideology, and Islamic obedience versus Christian individualism. For example, post-independence measures to exclude job-hungry educated southern Nigerians from civil service and teachings posts in the North for which few Hausa are qualified, were based not only on a desire not to be dominated by other regions but also on a rejection of the values which the educated southerners represent and might propagate. The overproduction of achieving individuals in southern Nigeria and their underproduction in the North thus result not simply in a problem of ethnic allocation of jobs but in a confrontation of contradictory ideologies of modernization and authority. This confrontation played an important part in the Ibo officers' revolt of 1966, which was inspired by sentiments similar to those of Chike Obi described in chapter 7.

The Yoruba, in their intermediate position on these dimensions of individual disposition, have been pulled in both directions. The Yoruba ethnic group contains within it individuals who are among the most Westernized and attitudinally modern in tropical Africa, but it also includes a large rural population which has had to change little in order to survive effectively in the contemporary period and which is still strongly oriented toward traditional patterns of leadership as represented by the *obas* (kings) and chiefs. For a while the Yoruba were able to operate as something of a political unit, but since early 1962 they have been torn by a severe political schism. What is notable from the viewpoint of this study is that the schism increasingly took on the flavor of a fundamental ideological conflict. Despite numerous countertrends, the main thrust of the split involved one faction appealing to traditional and less educated elements in the population, whereas the other gained support from modernizing intellectuals, professionals, and urban militants. Significantly, in 1964 the former became allied with the Hausa-dominated Northern Peoples' Congress, and the latter with the Ibo-dominated National Council of Nigerian Citizens. Thus the contemporary political behavior of the Yoruba, like their responses as measured in this study, shows them torn between the ideological poles represented by the more extreme Ibo and Hausa.

None of this will come as a surprise to the student of Nigerian politics. We present it in order to suggest that there is a consistent pattern of group differences revealed in unconscious imagery, explicit value-attitude formulations, educational achievement, and economic and political behavior. Although there are other ways of viewing it, we propose that the latter behaviors are the outcomes of culturally determined differences in the incidence of personality characteristics such as n Achievement and authoritarianism among the three ethnic groups. If this view is correct, then personality differences between ethnic groups are factors deserving more attention in the analysis of contemporary African social behavior than they have heretofore received.

APPENDIX A

THE USE OF DREAM REPORTS FOR THE CROSS-CULTURAL MEASUREMENT OF N ACHIEVEMENT

by

Eugene Strangman

In the McClelland-Atkinson method of scoring a story for n Achievement, the most important decision the scorer makes is whether or not the story contains Achievement Imagery. If it has been decided that the story does meet the criteria for scoring Achievement Imagery, the story is then scored for a variety of other categories of response. These responses correspond to the problem-solving sequence commonly used as a model in the analysis of overt behavior. Among these are statements of the need to achieve, instrumental acts directed toward achievement, obstacles to be overcome, anticipations of success or failure, and positive or negative affective reactions accompanying the success or failure of the enterprise. One is able to obtain an estimate of the strength of a subject's motivation to achieve by counting the number of such achievement-related categories in the set of stories collected from him. The sum of these categories is a rough measure of the individual's motive to achieve.[1]

The basic tool, then, for obtaining a measure of the strength of individual achievement motivation is this scoring system applied to individually produced fantasy.[2] The measure was developed on stories told by male college students. It has, however, been successfully

[1] For a complete description of the development of the measure of n Achievement, cf. D. C. McClelland *et al., The Achievement Motive* (New York: Appleton-Century-Crofts, Inc., 1953).

[2] The numerical score assigned to a story is as follows: If scored Unrelated Imagery, the score is —1; if scored Doubtful Achievement Imagery, the score is 0; if scored Achievement Imagery, one point is given for that and for each subcategory which is scored. Thus the potential score for any one story can vary from —1 to 11.

applied to stories told by male high-school students [3] and to stories collected from Navajo adolescent males.[4] Studies conducted in a number of other cultures produced much the same result.[5]

The method devised has been shown to be amazingly flexible. It has been successfully applied to other types of fantasy material, such as folk tales, stories appearing in children's readers, and literary productions. This application to collective fantasy was made in order to obtain *n* Achievement scores for cultural groups as a whole. Examples of such work are reported by Friedman and McClelland,[6] Child, Storm, and Veroff,[7] Parker, [8] McClelland,[9] Bradburn and Berlew.[10] It had not been previously applied to dreams.

The rationale for attempting to measure levels of achievement motivation in the three Nigerian ethnic groups is presented in chapter 5, but may be summarized as follows: Since the achievement motive is assumed to be a transcultural dimension of motivation, since motives have been shown to affect fantasy of which dreams are a form, and since the manifest content of dreams has been shown to reveal the motivations of the dreamer and the impact of the culture upon the individual, it was felt that we could legitimately expect to find evidence of achievement motivation in nighttime dream reports.

To apply the McClelland scoring system to dream reports necessitated first observing some of the major differences between dream reports and TAT stories. Chief among these is the fact that the dream reporter is invariably involved as a character in the dream he is reporting, whereas the subject telling a TAT story is rarely if ever involved as a character in the story he tells. In scoring a TAT

[3] J. A. Veroff, "Projective Measure of the Achievement Motivation of Adolescent Males and Females." Unpublished honors thesis, Wesleyan University, 1950. Cited in McClelland *et al., op. cit.*

[4] E. L. Lowell, "A Methodological Study of Projectively Measured Achievement Motivation." Unpublished Master's thesis, Wesleyan University. Cited in McClelland *et. al., op. cit.*

[5] D. C. McClelland, *The Achieving Society* (Princeton: Van Nostrand, 1961).

[6] D. C. McClelland and G. A. Friedman, "A Cross-Cultural Study of the Relationship between Child-Training Practices and Achievement Motivation Appearing in Folk Tales," in G. E. Swanson, T. M. Newcomb, and E. L. Hartley, *Readings in Social Psychology* (New York: Henry Holt & Co., 1952).

[7] I. L. Child, T. Storm, and J. Veroff, in "Achievement Themes in Folktales Relating to Socialization Practice," ed. J. W. Atkinson, *Motives in Fantasy, Action, and Society* (Princeton: Van Nostrand, 1958), pp. 479–92.

[8] Seymour Parker, "Motives in Eskimo and Ojibwa Mythology," *Ethnology*, I, No. 4 (1962), pp. 516–23.

[9] D. C. McClelland, *The Achieving Society.*

[10] N. M. Bradburn and D. E. Berlew, "Need for Achievement and English Industrial Growth," *Economic Development and Cultural Change*, X, No. 1 (1961), pp. 8–20.

story, if any one of the characters is involved in some competition with a standard of excellence, the inference is made that the subject is manifesting some need to achieve. In scoring dream reports, this inference is made only if the dream reporter himself is engaged in competition with a standard of excellence.

Second, dream reports are often more confused and less logical than consciously fabricated TAT stories. This might well be expected from the often alogical and fantastic material contained in a dream. This contributes to the difficulty in making the finer discriminations necessary in scoring Achievement Imagery subcategories. The manual used to score the dream reports appears at the end of this appendix, and may be compared with the manual for scoring TAT stories which appear in Atkinson, *Motives in Fantasy, Action and Society,* chapter 12. All the criteria proposed for the major categories (Unrelated Imagery, Doubtful Achievement Imagery, and Achievement Imagery) were accepted as published. The adaptation consisted mainly in setting up some conventions, consistent with the criteria, to guide the scorer in scoring the dream reports; after the initial reliability study, the subcategories were omitted and are not presented in the manual.

Two types of reliability, intrarater and interrater, were computed. To determine the interrater reliability of the measure, one of my colleagues [11] interested in learning the system, was engaged to score a random sample of dream reports. A training sample of sixty dream reports was drawn. After study of the manual and consultation with the author, he made his ratings. Frequent conferences were held to solve problems in scoring. Following this training sample, a random sample of 154 dream reports was drawn, which constituted the reliability sample. The most crucial decision to be made in scoring is whether or not the report meets the criteria for scoring Achievement Imagery. The two scorers reached an agreement of 87 per cent on the scoring of Achievement Imagery.[12] The percentage of agreement in scoring the subcategories was, however, substantially lower. Consequently, it was not possible to obtain an estimate of individual level of *n* Achievement from the dream reports. By not using the subcategories in the analysis, the job of rating each dream narrative was reduced to determining whether or not it contained Achievement Imagery according to the criteria in the manual. Computation of a Phi correlation coefficient between the two raters' scorings yielded a Phi $= .848$. This is significant beyond the .001 level. That it was not possible to obtain an estimate

[11] Leonard Unterberger.
[12] The percentage of agreement was computed by dividing the number of times the category was agreed upon times two by the total number of times the category was scored by the two scorers.

of individual level of n Achievement was in some ways disappointing, but not totally unexpected. There may be several reasons for the low percentage of agreement on Achievement Imagery subcategories. The nature of the data themselves may be responsible. Dream reports are generally more confused than TAT stories. In dreams, there is little regard for logical progression of thought as we commonly know it in secondary process thinking. The dreamer is reporting an event as he has experienced it; he is making little attempt to fabricate a coherent story. In TAT stories, as gathered by McClelland *et al.*, guiding questions are provided to enhance greatly the possibility of getting a logical, coherent story. In a dream the subject frequently jumps from one situation to the next with abandon. Thus the presentation is confused, and the criteria are more difficult to apply with precision.

Furthermore, in these data there was a lack of precision in the use of language. This is undoubtedly due to the fact that English is not the native language of these subjects. Because the criteria are heavily dependent on language, such lack of precision could have been partly responsible for the inability of the two scorers to make the finer discriminations consistently.

An intrarater scoring reliability check was conducted about seven months after the original scoring of the reports. A random sample of 129 reports was rescored. The agreement on scoring Achievement Imagery was 95.5 per cent.

On the basis of the above results it would seem that the scoring system is reasonably reliable, at least in the recognition of whether or not Achievement Imagery is present or absent. It remains for future studies to determine whether the Achievement Imagery subcategories can be reliably scored to permit an estimate of individual level of n Achievement.

Although reliability of any measure is extremely important, the usefulness of the measure is dependent upon how valid it is. The type of validity offered for this measure is construct validity. On the basis of a knowledge of the ethnographic data and firsthand knowledge of the groups involved, the senior author made predictions as to the way in which these three ethnic groups should be ordered in terms of the amount of Achievement Imagery manifested. He predicted that the frequency of Achievement Imagery should be in the following order (from most to least): Ibo, Southern Yoruba, Northern Yoruba, Hausa. The data supported these predictions in detail. More detailed results appear in chapter 5.

At this point, the universal validity of the measure is far from being demonstrated. There does seem to be evidence for construct validity. The question still remains, however, as to whether the results obtained in this study are unique to the groups investigated. Before this question can be answered satisfactorily, similar studies on different cultural groups will have to be carried out. Furthermore, do the results obtained with this measure compare favorably with the results of a measure of more widely accepted validity — for example, the TAT measure? Is it possible to measure other motives? To establish more general validity, a whole series of studies should be undertaken.

At this point, the question might be legitimately raised as to what advantage, if any, such a measure of motivation would have over the TAT or collective fantasy measures that would justify such a program of research. Two arguments seem strong enough to justify such a program. The most compelling reason is that if successfully established as a measure of motivation it would offer a solution to the problem of stimulus equivalence in cross-cultural research. Within a homogeneous culture, a given stimulus will almost certainly possess the same meaning for all people living in that culture. In a heterogeneous culture such as ours, however, the problem of the meaning of a test stimulus to different persons taking the test becomes acute. The test stimuli take on different meanings to persons with very different cultural backgrounds. This problem is magnified when applied to different cultures around the globe. Constructing a different set of stimuli for each culture is a partial but not totally satisfactory way of dealing with the problem. There is no way of knowing whether the various sets of stimuli are tapping the same motivational system at the same level. Dreams, however, seem to be a universal phenomenon. Consequently, people of all cultures can be expected to have had the experience of dreaming. Asking a subject to report a dream or a series of dreams is a different task from asking him to respond to a specific set of stimuli. In the former, he is reporting an experience over which he has little, if any, voluntary control; in the latter, he is asked to interpret a stimulus or set of stimuli and respond accordingly. By not having to respond to specific stimuli, the problems of stimulus equivalence are diminished and thus a prime source of cultural contamination is eliminated.

The second reason for carrying out research to establish the validity of this method has to do with sound procedures for studying modal personality or group differences in personality. The ideal way to determine the modal personality of a cultural group is to test a large sample of individuals from that group to obtain a picture of the ranging along a variety of personality dimensions extant in that culture. This is often a difficult task when individual administration of tests is involved. Furthermore, a minimal education level is necessary in order to respond to some of those tests.

Dreaming makes no such demands. Educated and uneducated alike dream. The only requirement necessary is the ability and willingness to report the dream experience. For the investigator, the time and effort needed to collect the data should be diminished.

MANUAL FOR SCORING *N* ACHIEVEMENT IN NIGHTTIME DREAM NARRATIVES

The scorer must first decide whether the dream narrative contains any reference to an achievement goal which would justify scoring the subcategories as achievement related. By achievement goal is meant success in competition with some standard of excellence. The goal of the dreamer in the dream narrative is to be successful in terms of competition with some standard of excellence. The individual may fail to achieve this goal, but the concern over competition with a standard of excellence still enables the scorer to identify the goal sought as an achievement goal. This is the generic definition of *n* Achievement to be used. In the definitions for scoring criteria which follow, it will become apparent that some types of imagery are included in which there is no explicit statement in the dream narrative concerning competition with a standard of excellence. For these particular criteria it is felt that the evidence is sufficient for a fairly safe inference that competition with a standard of excellence is implicitly involved.

Criteria for Achievement Imagery (AI)
1. *Competition with a Standard of Excellence*
   a. The dreamer is engaged in some competitive activity (other than pure instances of aggression) where winning or doing as well as or better than someone else is actually stated as the primary concern, for example, a boy who dreams himself competing against other boys in a swimming meet and trying hard to win would be scored AI since competition is directly involved.
   b. If the dreamer is engaged in some competitive activity (other than pure instances of aggression), but the desire to win or do as well as or better than others is not explicitly stated, then (1) affective concern over goal attainment and (2) some types of instrumental activity are considered as indicating that the desire to compete successfully with a standard of excellence is implicit in the dream narrative. Example of 1: "I was delirious with joy when I learned I had passed the examination." Example of 2: "I studied very hard to pass the examination for my certificate."

c. Sometimes the standard of excellence involves no competition with others, but does involve meeting the self-imposed requirements of good performance. In this instance, in order to score for AI, words are needed to the effect that a good job is wanted.

Distinction is made between statements of the intensity and quality of instrumental acts. Working hard or working fast would be evidence of concern over achievement only when excellence at the task demanded speed or intense effort. But a person may work hard to complete a task for reasons other than personal achievement; for example, "I dreamed that I worked hard on my homework," may indicate only that the individual wants to get it out of the way, and would not be scored AI. However, "I dreamed that I checked my calculus problems again and again before handing them in," implies concern with accuracy, a standard of excellence; in this instance, AI would be scored.

2. *Unique Accomplishment*

The dreamer is involved in or wants to accomplish something other than a run-of-the-mill task which will mark him as a personal success. Inventions, artistic creations, and other extraordinary accomplishments fulfill this criterion. There need be neither explicit statement of concern over the outcome nor a direct statement that a good job is wanted when the individual is working on a new invention or is in the process of doing something unique which will be generally accepted as a personal accomplishment. Dreams in which the dreamer sees himself as king or emir are not scored AI. This is a totally unrealistic ambition since these positions are ascribed, not achieved.

3. *Long-Term Involvement*

The dreamer is involved in attainment of a long-term achievement goal. Dreams of becoming an engineer, surgeon, or the like, are examples of career involvement which permit the inference of competition with a standard of excellence unless it is made explicit that another goal is primary—for example, personal security, owning and driving flashy cars, and so on.

If the dreamer is engaged in or concerned over the attainment of a limited achievement goal—that is, a specific task—it is scored AI when it can be shown that these limited or routine tasks are definitely related to a long term achievement goal.

Doubtful Achievement Imagery (TI)

Narratives containing some references to achievement but which fail to meet one of the criteria for Achievement Imagery are scored Doubtful Achievement Imagery (TI). The symbol T indicates that most frequently the narratives to be classified as doubtful are ones in which one of the characters is engaged in a commonplace task or solving a routine problem. Whenever there is doubt about whether or not one of the criteria for Achievement Imagery has been met, and when the narrative is not totally unrelated to achievement, it is classified TI.

More explicit criteria for scoring TI are the following.

1. If the dream concerns achievement or achievement striving on the part of people other than the dreamer, score TI since there is no evidence for affective involvement or competition with a standard of excellence on the part of the dreamer.

2. Dream narratives in which the dreamer sees himself as an emir or king are scored TI.

3. If the narrative is one in which the dreamer sees himself associating with eminent people, score TI. This might indicate a desire to attain such a position; when no explicit statement to this effect appears, it cannot, however, rightfully be scored AI.

4. Dreams in which the dreamer is struggling to get out of a potentially dangerous situation are not scored TI, but UI. Presumably the motive here is to protect oneself.

Unrelated Imagery (VI)

Narratives in which there is no reference to an achievement goal are scored unrelated imagery (UI).

Some General Criteria for Handling the Dream Narratives

1. Treat the entire written production as a whole, including statements leading up to the report of the dream itself as well as additional comments at the end of the dream report.

2. When two or more dreams on the same subject matter are reported in one dream narrative, as sometimes occurs in the accounts of recurrent dreams, treat the report as a single dream narrative.

3. In all instances where AI is scored, the dreamer himself must be the one engaged in striving for the achievement goal. Instances where other individuals are engaged in the achievement striving, the dreamer being an observer, are scored TI.

APPENDIX B

THE MEASUREMENT OF SOCIAL VALUES
IN WRITTEN ESSAYS

by

Leonard Unterberger

The purpose of this section is to present the method by which the written essays were analyzed in order to test the principal hypotheses of the study. We were interested in the degree to which respondents in the three ethnic groups saw obedience and achievement values as leading to success, and we wanted to measure them in a way that was reliable and valid.

One may question at the outset why a new technique for the measurement of values was required. A number of useful methods have been developed in the past several decades, among them Thurstone's [1] method of paired comparisons, and statement items developed to form Likert Scales. This latter approach characterizes the studies of achievement values in the United States by Rosen [2] and Strodtbeck.[3] The difficulties to be overcome in the application of these methods are similar, and are the familiar ones in cross-cultural research of discovering stimuli which have equivalent meanings for the groups being studied.[4] The required time, facilities, and familiarity with the diverse value systems of the groups being studied for the refinement of items for such scaling techniques were not available. An alternative strategy was to secure raw responses from the students, which took advantage of their common ability to

[1] L. L. Thurstone, *The Measurement of Values* (Chicago: University of Chicago Press, 1959), pp. 182–94.

[2] B. C. Rosen, "The Achievement Syndrome: A Psychocultural Dimension of Stratification," *American Sociological Review*, XXI (1956), pp. 203–11.

[3] F. L. Strodtbeck, "Family Interaction, Values and Achievement," in *Talent and Society*, eds. D. McClelland, A. L. Baldwin, U. Bronfenbrenner, and F. L. Strodtbeck (Princeton: Van Nostrand, 1958), pp. 135–94.

[4] R. R. Sears, "Transcultural Variables and Conceptual Equivalence," *Studying Personality Cross-Culturally*, ed. B. Kaplan (Evanston: Row Peterson, 1961), pp. 445–56.

use the English language as a medium of communication. Although the ethnic groups may vary in the ways in which they have assimilated and use the language, manifestations of these differences would at least be preserved in the response, available for study and control.

With the essays collected, a method for assessing the value-relevant content in them had to be chosen. The technique of content analysis seemed to afford the most adequate approach. The method provides an "objective, systematic and quantitative description of the manifest content of communication."[5]

Three systems of categories have been developed for the comprehensive analysis of values in written material. Each will be briefly reviewed to evaluate its chief advantages and its relevance to the hypotheses proposed earlier.

White's "Value Analysis"[6] was designed to secure an exhaustive description of value statements in written material. The system is divided into two broad areas: statements of specific goals organized under such headings as physiological, fearful, playful, and cognitive; and standards of evaluation, including major headings of moral, social, and egoistic standards. This system, presented as an exhaustive inventory of values in contemporary American society, comprises a total of fifty specific categories. White has applied different aspects of the system to the study of a novel[7] and to a body of propaganda and public opinion materials.[8] The chief advantage of this approach to the study of values lies in its flexibility. White has suggested a number of adaptations to fit the system to particular research objectives. The comprehensiveness of the system is, however, its chief limitation as well, since scope is attained at the expense of a more detailed exploration and definition of nuances of the proposed value categories.

Von Mering[9] has devised a system of content analysis categories for the assessment of value relevant consequences of the breadth and intensity of intercultural living. Four possible value realms are posited as constituting a "grammar of values." Two of the four realms are defined by their relative concreteness and restricted applicability. Contrasted to these realms are the comprehensive

[5] B. P. Berelson, *Content Analysis in Communication Research* (Glencoe: The Free Press, 1952), p. 8.

[6] R. K. White, *Value Analysis, the Nature and Use of the Method* (Society for the Psychological Study for Social Issues, 1951).

[7] R. K. White, "Black Boy: A Value Analysis," *Journal of Abnormal and Social Psychology*, XLII (1947), pp. 440-61.

[8] R. K. White, "Hitler, Roosevelt, and the Nature of War Propaganda," *Journal of Abnormal and Social Psychology*, XLIV (1949), pp. 157–74.

[9] O. von Mering, *A Grammar of Human Values* (Pittsburgh: University of Pittsburgh Press, 1961).

and inclusive value realms, comprised of abstract values which comprehend the totality of an immediate experience and imply that the standards of the values transcend the givens of immediate experience. Characteristic of these value domains are statements advocating mutuality, reciprocity, interdependence, and the recognition of human differences. The grammar of values was devised for the analysis of transcripts of problem-centered discussions among residents in an area offering frequent opportunity for intercultural contact. This system of categories affords a distinction among value responses along the universalistic-particularistic dimension proposed by Parsons,[10] a distinction particularly relevant to von Mering's hypotheses. Application of this system, without major revision and amplification of its categories to conform to the hypotheses relevant to this study, seemed, however, an indirect and not particularly fruitful approach.

McClelland[11] reports a scoring scheme for the study of values in stories written for children. The analytic approach is based on a distinction between the norms and values surrounding an individual's obligation to himself and the norms and values governing his relationship to society. The analysis is undertaken from two points of view: from the perspective of the action sequence undertaken by the hero or central figure in the story, and the actions implicating other representatives of the social order. Categories of analysis for the hero include impinging influences, his status, response to outer influence, the object of that response, outcome of the sequence, and evaluation of the hero in terms of achieved or ascribed status. The interaction sequence, studied from the point of view of others, comprehends the sources of interaction pressure, the means of exerting pressure, the hero's motives for interacting, and the outcome from alter's point of view. The set of categories was devised to assess the relevance of a large number of theoretical formulations regarding the origins of pressure for economic growth. Although a number of categories are relevant to the hypotheses under consideration, these were found to be duplicated in the McClelland-Atkinson scoring system for n Achievement. Their inclusion is reflected in the adaptations of that set of content categories for the measurement of achievement values.

Each of these reported value analyses systems was devised to satisfy criteria determined by an immediate research problem. The categories these researchers established were relevant to hypotheses

[10] T. Parsons, E. A. Shils, "Values, Motives and Systems of Action," *Toward a General Theory of Action*, eds. T. Parsons and E. A. Shils (Cambridge, Mass.: Harvard University Press, 1951), pp. 47–275.

[11] D. C. McClelland, *The Achieving Society* (Princeton: Van Nostrand, 1961).

being tested and provided direct links between theory and data. A similar procedure was followed in the elaboration of content analysis categories for the present study. Although the specific set of categories employed for this study are without exact precedent, the methodological framework on which they are based is a familiar one.

The first task was to devise sets of content analysis categories for the study of achievement and obedience-social-compliance value motifs. Three criteria guided the development of these instruments: they should provide a direct bridge between the hypotheses and the written essays; the unit of analysis should refer to some stable characteristic of the essays; and, finally, the measures should be independent.

The first criterion directed the selection of the McClelland-Atkinson system for n Achievement as a point of departure for the development of the achievement values measure. The derivation of categories for the obedience-social-compliance device was guided by a description of authority patterns among the three ethnic groups. From this description a definition of the domains of deferential behavior was tentatively developed.

Several characteristics of the essays dictated the selection of the unit of analysis. Inferences were derived from a random sample of thirty essays, masked for ethnic group identity, which had been separated from the total sample and used only for purposes of devising the measures. This sample of essays was found to have marked variability of length of phrase, sentence, paragraph, as well as total essay. There was little consistent use of grammatical conventions. Motifs thought to be relevant to the then approximately conceptualized categories were noted and found to vary prodigiously in length. For example, a student might say, "A boy must obey his parents," or this theme might be elaborated extensively, though not necessarily sequentially, in the essay. The possibility of counting the frequency of occurrence of value motifs was considered but rejected when it was observed that variation in motif length would not be accounted for by this procedure. There was the additional possibility that consistent differences in styles of compositions might be reflected in such a measure. It seemed important to avoid repeated scoring dictated by the observed frequent and sometimes lengthy interpolations of value motifs not relevant to the values being studied. These observations and considerations led to the selection of the uniform typed line, averaging ten words, as the unit of analysis.

To satisfy the third criterion, it was decided that the content analysis systems should be developed independently and that the essays should be rated separately for achievement and obedience-social-compliance values.

There remained the process of refining the achievement content analysis system. Provisional definitions of the categories were established, and the trial set of essays was scored by the author; two other raters scored half of the set each. The achievement values categories found relevant to the essays were retained, and those not used for these ratings were excluded from the system. The nurturant press category was excluded, and other categories were refined to emphasize self-reliance in instrumental behavior. This was an attempt to provide a clearer distinction between the achievement and obedience-social-compliance dimensions.

At this stage of the work, it was observed that the content of the two essays written by each subject overlapped, with the distinction between a definition of a successful man and how to become a successful man not being maintained. A decision was made to combine both essays. This provided the advantage of increasing the amount of material on which the final score for each respondent would be based. The combined essays served as the unit of record for each subject.

Random samples of sixty-five records were drawn from both the Southern Yoruba and the Ibo populations. The entire research sample of Hausa, Ibo, and Yoruba records was masked for ethnic group identification and randomly ordered. A selection of the remaining essays was combined with Southern Yoruba and a group of girl's responses to provide five sets of twenty-five essays for training purposes. These essays were also masked for ethnic group identification.

Two training sets of essays were rated by the author and an assistant. Percentages of interrater agreement [12] were 64 and 60 respectively. Essays containing the greatest disagreement were reviewed. Three sources of error seemed to account for differences in judgments: deflections of attention, differing judgments about where motifs began and ended, and disagreements in interpretation. The last two sources of error indicated need for further revision of the scoring system and scoring conventions. Both the scoring criteria and conventions were refined in the direction of more precise specification of issues relevant to the judgment process. Scoring of the third and fourth training sets resulted in measures of agreement of 89 per cent and 86 per cent respectively. The research sample was then scored, one judge proceeding from the first to the last subject, and the other beginning with the last.

When the scoring of achievement values was completed, the obedience-social-compliance instrument was developed. The defini-

---

[12] The percentage of agreement was computed by dividing the number of agreements times two by the sum of the number of agreements times two and the number of disagreements.

tion of domains of deferential behavior was elaborated inductively by referring to essays in the training sets for relevant examples. Scoring criteria were developed with specific reference to the description of the means employed to attain success goals. Conventions established for scoring of achievement-value motifs were used without revision. Scores were obtained from three training sets consisting of ten essays each. These sets did not include those used for the development of the instrument. Interrater reliability, as measured by percentage of agreement, was 89, 85, and 92 respectively. The research sample was then scored following the same procedures established in the scoring of achievement-value motifs.

The subjects of this study were drawn from the larger sample of male students described in chapter 4. The entire sample of Hausa students was included and matched by an equal number of respondents drawn randomly from Ibo and Southern Yoruba ethnic groups. The Northern Yoruba were excluded from this analysis because it was not thought to be worth the effort of coding their essays without having a specific basis for predicting their responses. A comparison of the subsample with the larger sample on the independent variables of age, grade placement, mother's and father's education, and religion indicates that the sample employed for this research is similar in every respect to the larger sample.

With the essays scored, an assessment of interrater reliability was made. Measures of the percentage of agreement for the 195 essays in the sample were calculated for both instruments. The interrater reliability for scores of achievement value motifs was 95 per cent, and for the analysis of obedience-social-compliance, 97 per cent. Phi coefficients for these judgments were .66 and .70 respectively. Both correlations are significant beyond the .001 level. It should be noted that the measure of interrater agreement is reported in gross terms rather than in terms of agreement on each category.

The measure of preoccupation with achievement values was derived by taking the arithmetic mean of the scores assigned by each rater to a record. The same procedure was followed on obedience-social-compliance scores for each subject. Table 11 presents the means and standard deviations of the raw scores for each group on each measure. Two questions can be raised from the results presented here. Given these data, can we assume that the distribution of scores would approach normality with increased sampling? The fact that the modal score was zero for all groups on both measures suggests that the skewness is an unexpected artifact of the scoring system. Thus, increasing the size of the sample was not considered a feasible approach to correcting the non-normal property of

TABLE 11

MEANS AND STANDARD DEVIATIONS OF RAW SCORES FOR
ACHIEVEMENT AND OBEDIENCE-SOCIAL-COMPLIANCE
VALUES BY ETHNIC GROUPS

	MEAN	STANDARD DEVIATION
	ACHIEVEMENT	
Ibo	8.42	9.47
Yoruba	9.58	10.97
Hausa	7.12	8.71
	OBEDIENCE-SOCIAL-COMPLIANCE	
Ibo	4.69	5.18
Yoruba	5.18	5.01
Hausa	7.25	6.55

the distribution. The second question concerns the homogeneity of variances for the groups. Most statistics assuming a normal distribution of scores assume by implication that the variances of the grouped scores are homogeneous; this assumption was satisfied for the present data by a procedure reported below.

Another difficulty was length. As mentioned earlier, the essays varied in length, and it was thought that the raw values scores might be correlated with the lengths of the essays. To test this hypothesis, every sixth essay was selected from the random list of achievement scores, and a Pearson-product-moment correlation computed to assess the presence and strength of the relationship. A similar computation was performed for the OSC measure. The correlation between raw scores and essay length was .33 for achievement and .28 for OSC. A correction for length was thus required.

The entire body of essays was arranged by length and divided into successive fifths (for example, the shortest fifth, the next shortest fifth, and so on). The raw achievement and OSC scores in each fifth were converted to Z scores. This normalizing procedure effectively eliminated the correlation, and at the same time somewhat reduced the skewness of the distribution of scores. One further conquence of this transformation of scores remains to be considered. The modal score (0) for each group, now transformed to Z scores, ranged from -1.29 to $-.82$ for OSC and from -1.83 to $-.82$ for achievement. Both sample size and this artifactually introduced difference among scores of the same magnitude eliminated the application of rank order statistics. An analysis of variance technique was chosen to take into account the absolute magnitude of the differences among scores introduced by the Z score transformation.

The analysis of variance technique employed to analyze the grouped scores had the further advantage of demonstrating that the variances among the groups on both measures were in fact homogeneous. The results of the general multivariate analysis of variance [13] are presented in Table 12. An examination of line 4 in the table indicates that the hypothesis that the variances of the three groups are homogeneous is supported. We can conclude that the homogeneity of variances criterion is satisfied. Line 5 of the table

TABLE 12

ETHNIC GROUP MEANS AND STANDARD DEVIATIONS OF
Z SCORES FOR TWO VALUE DIMENSIONS

	ACH		OSC	
	MEAN	SD.	MEAN	SD.
1. Ibo	− 0.10	.86	− 0.20	.83
2. Yoruba	0.92	1.00	− 0.09	.94
3. Hausa	− 0.00	1.12	0.29	1.06

GENERAL ANALYSIS

4. $H_1 = M = 10.3$ $F_{918763}^{6} = 1.69$ $.75 < p < .90$

5. $H_2 = \wedge = .94$ $F_{382}^{4} = 2.90$ $.01 < p < .025$

conveys the result of the second hypothesis, that the group means are equal. The F ratio attains significance between .01 and .025 levels, permitting the rejection of the statement that the group means are equal. One-tail T tests were employed to locate the differences among the group means. These results are presented in tables 7 and 8 in chapter 6.

A number of major assumptions are implicit in this content analysis study. The first is that the meanings ascribed by the content analyst to written material by assigning it to categories corresponds to the meanings intended by the student essayists; it was necessary to proceed on the assumption that the words and phrases employed by the students would convey the intended meaning to the raters. To guard against violations of this assumption, a convention was established which precluded scoring when the meaning was unclear. Further precautions were taken by having the content rated by two independent judges. The measure of interrater agreement reflects

[13] W. W. Cooley and P. R. Lohnes, *Multivariate Procedures for the Behavioral Sciences* (New York: Wiley, 1962), pp. 60–87.

the degree to which the content analysis systems were employed objectively.

The second assumption employed in this research is that the relative extent of preoccupation with specified content in the essays is an adequate measure of the importance of the value orientation for the ethnic groups. This assumption underlies the predictions that Ibo, Hausa, and Southern Yoruba students would be differentially concerned with achievement and obedience-social-compliance values. To the extent that we have been able to confirm the specific predictions, independent support of this assumption is provided. The correctness of prediction provides the only indication of validity for this measure.

The two content analysis measures were developed in the absence of other more direct means to assess the social values studied here. This technique is arduous and time-consuming. It does, however, provide an empirical approach to the study of differences in values among ethnic groups when these groups share a common medium of expression or when translation of written samples of behavior is possible. The chief advantage of the technique is to be found in the freedom provided subjects for expressing their value orientations and elaborating them in their own words. Their responses are available for subsequent analysis, thereby permitting an assessment of the interpretation given by subjects to the stimulus conditions.

What we have presented is an application of the projective method for the study of intrapsychic dimensions of personality to the study of transpersonal personality characteristics, the social values espoused by respondents of different ethnic groups. This technique may prove to be extremely useful for exploratory cross-cultural studies of social values. More refined instruments, such as attitude scales, may be derived from such exploratory content analyses.

MANUAL FOR THE SCORING OF VALUE MOTIFS

The scorer's task is to identify the presence, location, and extent of elaboration of value motifs in essays. Values are also termed goals or wants, and are seen as socially desirable. For the purpose of this research, the value motif is defined as a group of words or phrases which serve as a guide for overt behavior. The guides can be prescriptive, stating desired behaviors and goals, or they can be proscriptive, indicating behaviors and goals to be avoided. Both types of statements are included in this scoring system.

The scorer's first concern is with the presence and extent of elaboration of value motifs. The consolidated essay is the unit of record, and within it, the lines on each page are defined as the subunit in the measure of elaboration. In preparation for scoring, the manuals should be reread in full, and then, with the summary of criteria at hand, the first reading of an essay can begin. The first reading focuses on determining whether relevant value motifs appear in the essay, and the context in which they occur should be noted. The second reading is directed toward deciding whether or not words and phrases are relevant to the criteria and scoring.

The decision that a value motif is scorable depends on the answers to several questions. The question of whether there is enough information to permit scoring with sureness depends on judgments based on the immediate context in which the motif appears. The specific questions to be put to possibly relevant motifs are stated in the summary of criteria, but the following general rule holds. If the information is insufficient to convince the scorer of the correctness of scoring a given subunit, he should refrain from scoring. If meaning has to be inferred from the sequence, or if the expression of the motif is not sufficiently clear, the unit should not be scored.

The determination of elaboration is made by reading from the scoring template the lines which include the motif statement. Lines may precede cue words or follow them, depending on whether the writer opens with his main point or closes with it. In both instances it is difficult to determine the boundaries of elaboration. A few guides may help.

1. Examples which serve to elaborate a motif are always included.

2. Examples which serve to specify the meaning of a motif are always included.

3. Statements which are opposites of the motif and of the relevant criterion (for example, hard work and laziness) are often used to establish the boundaries of meaning by indicating what is not relevant to the central idea being developed. These statements are included in the measure of elaboration when they serve to reinforce or clarify a motif.

4. If an example introduces ambiguity — confuses more than it clarifies — then scoring is not justified.

5. Words or phrases which occur within a definable motif are excluded from the measure of elaboration when they contradict the motif being elaborated. This may result in breaking up into segments what may possibly be a related motif. Such segments can be scored only if they extend for at least one line.

6. When a motif is continued from one paragraph to another, continuous numbering of lines may misrepresent the extent to which the motif is elaborated. When this occurs, the extent of elaboration in each paragraph should be noted separately.

The mechanics of scoring for location and extent of elaboration are as follows.

1. A motif beginning and ending on one line — line 10, for example — is scored 10. Elaboration is one line.

2. A motif beginning on one line and extending to another full line is scored 10-11. Elaboration is two lines.

3. A motif beginning on a line and extending beyond a second line to include more than two words of a third line (articles are excluded from the word count) is scored 10-12. Elaboration is 2.5 lines.

To avoid cataloguing word sequences of descriptive attributes that may be relevant to a criterion, a general rule to follow is that elaborations of less than one line are not scored. Elaboration extending more than one line may be scored only if the descriptive list is entirely consistent with the criteria and does not introduce other classes of descriptive value terms (for example, moral ones).

The Scoring of Achievement Motifs

Achievement motifs are conveyed by a variety of content. Common to them is active striving toward a distant, difficult to attain, and highly valued goal. The goal may be seen as attainable or fear of failure may be expressed, but the desirability of the goal, the striving directed toward goal attainment, still permits it to be defined as an achievement goal.

The specific criteria

1. *Competition with a standard of excellence*

Statements referring to doing as well as or better than others provides guides for scoring by this criterion. For example, a line which includes a statement about "getting the best grade in school" or "getting the best job" would be scored, since competition is explicit. Statements referring to successful competition in battle and other group activities are excluded from scoring.

2. *Self-imposed standards of excellence*

Occasionally, the attainment of success does not involve explicit competition with others but does involve meeting a self-imposed standard. In these instances, mention of that standard is required for scoring. For example, the statement "If a man is to be a carpenter, he ought to master the skills he will need" is scored by this criterion.

3. *Self-imposed goals*

The establishment of goals by the individual himself rather than the acceptance of goals imposed or offered by others defines this criterion. The notion here is of the self-selection of a goal from a number of alternative possibilities. If teachers', parents', or supervisors' directions are accepted, then the statement is not scored. Statements indicating that the imposition of goals by others must be opposed would be scored. Similarly, statements referring to self-reliance in goal selection and in goal-directed striving would be scored. If the origin of a goal is unstated, assume that the goal is self-selected.

4. *Long-term involvement*

Success is by definition a distant goal. Long-term involvement in achieving the goal is implicit. Scoring for this criterion is warranted if specific mention is made of planning of an individual's own activities to achieve a goal, as distinguished from the ability to plan and organize the work of others in a joint enterprise. The latter is not scored. Planning for day-to-day maintenance is to be distinguished from long-range planning, with only the latter included in the scoring.

Long-term involvement is most clearly seen in motifs emphasizing striving toward an elusive goal rather than actual goal attainment.

5. *Instrumental activity*

Descriptions of overt behaviors leading to the attainment of an achievement goal are considered instrumental to goal attainment and are scored. There may be a statement of goal-directed activity in the essay independent of the description of the goal and of desires to attain the goal.

The most frequently encountered theme is the motif of hard work which falls within this category. It is scored only if

   a. there is an explicit standard of excellence against which the work is being measured, and

   b. the work is presented as a direct means to goal attainment.

Simple mention of hard work is insufficient for scoring, as is work directed toward solving the routine problems of existence (the provision of food, shelter, and care for dependents). Work done under the direction of others or resulting from the demands of parents, teachers, and supervisors is excluded from scoring.

Mention that education is a prerequisite to success is scored only if there is a recognition that skills are learned and that the employment of these skills provides the means to goal attainment. If education is viewed as a means of developing latent talents or abilities that are instrumental to goal attainment, then scoring is warranted if these talents and abilities are seen as being employed in striving to attain the goal. The distinction being made here is between active striving toward making or attaining a place for oneself and developing abilities which permit one to fit into an occupational niche. Schooling also teaches the amenities of social interaction which may be seen as relevant to goal attainment, but such incidental learnings are not scored.

6. *Obstacles*

Goal-directed striving does not always proceed uninterruptedly. Obstacles may be confronted, either in the world or within the person. The desire to procrastinate is an example of the latter. Patient endurance of these obstacles to goal-directed striving is to be distinguished from active, persistent striving to overcome the obstacles. Only the latter is scored.

A SUMMARY LIST OF CRITERION AND CRITICAL QUESTIONS

1. *Competition with a standard of excellence*

   a. Is competition with others for a valued goal implicitly or explicitly mentioned? If so, the motif is scored.

   b. Excluded from scoring are competition in battle and other forms of group competition.

2. *Self-imposed standards of excellence*

Is a self-imposed standard of excellence — for example, "a good job" — mentioned? If so, the motif is scored.

3. *Self-imposed achievement goals*

   a. Is the success goal self-selected, or is it offered or imposed by parents, teachers, or supervisors? Only the former motifs are scored.

   b. Is there an explicit statement of self-reliance in goal selection? If so, the motif is scored.

   c. Statements indicating that the imposition of goals by others must be opposed would be scored.

4. *Long-term involvement*

   a. Is specific mention made of planning activities to achieve a goal? If so, the motif is scored.

   b. A distinction is to be made between day-to-day planning and long-range planning. Only the latter is scored.

5. *Instrumental activity*

   a. Is there an explicit standard of excellence against which instrumental activity is being measured? If so, the motif is scored.

   b. Is instrumental activity seen as a direct means to goal attainment? To success? If so, it is scored.

   c. Is instrumental activity determined by the demands of others or self-determined? Only the latter is scored.

d. Does mention of education as a prerequisite for goal attainment include the recognition that skills are learned? If so, the motif is scored.

e. Is the educational experience seen as a way of developing abilities which fit a person for an occupational niche, or is it seen as an experience which develops skills and abilities which are employed in active striving toward a goal? Only the latter motif is scored.

6. *Obstacles*

Can a distinction be made between patient waiting for obstacles to disappear and active, persistent striving to overcome obstacles in the world or in the self? Only the latter is scored.

The Scoring of Obedience-Social-Compliance Value Motifs

The obedience-social-compliance dimension embraces those value motifs which establish a range of means to attain a goal — the topic of the essays is success. Goal states are more frequently specified, and include the maintenance of friendly relationships, the provision of daily necessities, a happy home and family life, self-satisfaction, and happiness, to name a few. The wide range of goal states does not, however, permit sufficient precision to serve as criterion for scoring obedience-social-compliance motifs. For this reason, the means employed to attain these desired but diverse goals are used to determine the presence or absence of value motifs relevant to the obedience-social-compliance dimension.

Obedience-social-compliance value motifs are defined as those statements indicating that success or the goal state is attained through the subordination of self to the direction, control, or tutelage of others. Subordination is valued — that is, it is advanced as an effective and socially desirable means to an end. The appearance of statements relevant to this dimension permits the inference of value unless the statements are explicitly negated — for example, "A boy should listen to the advice of elders, but then think about what is right or wrong."

The subordination of self may occur with reference to those in authority — for example, parents, elders, teachers, and superiors — or with peers. Self-subordination may have reference to subordinates as well. In addition, there are a number of general agents toward which subordination may be expressed, including authority in general, public opinion or some segment of it, the law, regulations, and the traditional customs of a people.

The Specific Criteria
I. Obedience-social-compliance to superordinates
A. Superordinates include all those individuals seen in positions of authority or in a predominant age-status grouping (parents, elders, teachers, or supervisors). Subordination of self is reflected in statements advocating the unquestioning obedience and conformance to the expectation, demands, requests, or suggestions issuing from these sources. It is important to distinguish statements advocating unquestioning obedience from those which explicitly impose conditions upon such obedience. Examples of the former include:
1. "A successful man keeps the rules of his employer and carries out his duties."
2. "To be a success you have to do what you are asked by your teacher the best way you are able to."
3. "A boy must be obedient and helpful to his parents."
Statements espousing conditional obedience are exemplified by:
1. "A boy should listen to his parents when he thinks they are right."
2. "Elders' advice should be listened to, but a boy has to decide what is good and what is not."
Qualifications are often introduced. For example:
1. "A boy should try to follow the advice of his parents to the best of his ability."
2. "Sometimes the advice of elders should be followed."
The advocacy of unquestioning obedience is always scored, as are qualified obedience motifs. Explicit statements of conditional obedience are not scored.
B. Another expression of obedience-social-compliance is to be found in motifs referring the emulation to respected persons, parents, elders, teachers, or historical figures. Such statements are scored when the emulation advocated is uncritical and unquestioning. It is also scored when there is evidence that no choice has been made among a number of persons or attributes of persons. In summary, motifs indicating indiscriminate copying of others are scored.
C. Obedience-social-compliance is to be found in motifs referring to simple respect for the persons or opinions and judgments of those in authority. Motifs explicitly indicating that respect for those in authority is instrumental to success or characteristic of a successful person are scored. Simple mention of respect for those in authority is not sufficient for scoring.
II. Obedience-social-compliance to peers
A. A peer is defined as anyone perceived as equal to the es-

sayist in position or age status. Compliance to the demands, expectations, requests, and suggestions issuing from these sources is scored if the desire is imposed by the other, and the compliant response is seen as a means to goal attainment, either explicitly or implicitly. For example, "To stay on good terms, a boy should do what his friends want him to do" would be scored by this criterion.

B. A distinction is to be made between compliance and social accommodation. The latter refers to a process of give and take, implying mutuality in the regulation of a relationship, while the former refers to the subordination of self to the desires of others. Thus, for example, "A boy should learn the likes and dislikes of others so he would know how to deal with them" would not be scored.

C. A distinction is to be made between motifs emphasizing susceptibility to influence by others and compliance to the desires of others. The following example would not be scored: "A boy must avoid bad company if he is to be successful."

III. Obedience-social-compliance to subordinates

Motifs which state that a person should be attentive to and regulate his behavior in accordance with the expectations of those in subordinate positions is scored. Thus, for example, "A businessman will work so that those under him will be blessed with his management" would be scored.

IV. Some general referents

A. Motifs which stress unquestioning obedience to authority in general are scored.

B. Motifs which stress the importance of attending to and conforming to general public opinion or some segment of it are scored.

C. Motifs which elaborate on the importance of respect for or obedience to the law, regulations, or traditional customs of a people are scored. Excluded are general references to patriotism and loyalty to country, but the explicit subordination of self to the good of the country would be scored.

D. Motifs which stress the importance of obedience training in childhood are scored.

E. Motifs which elaborate religious themes — for example, respect for or obedience to God's will — are excluded from scoring.

A Summary List of Criteria

I. To superordinates:

A. Unquestioning obedience to the desires of those seen in positions of authority is scored. Qualified (sometimes, try to obey, and so on) but unquestioning obedience motifs are also scored. Not scored are those motifs which impose conditions upon such obedience.

B. Emulation of respected persons is scored when motifs permit the inference that the emulation is undiscriminating.

C. Motifs referring to respect for persons in authority, when seen as instrumental to success or characteristic of a successful person, are scored.

II. To peers:

A. Motifs referring to obedience-social-compliance to the desires of an age mate are scored when this behavior is seen as instrumental to goal attainment.

B. A distinction is to be made between compliance and accommodation. Only the former is scored.

C. A distinction is to be made between motifs emphasizing susceptibility to influence by others and compliance to the desires of others. Only the latter is scored.

III. To subordinates:

Motifs which state that a person should regulate his behavior in accordance with the expectations of those in subordinate positions are scored.

IV. General referents:

A. Motifs which stress unquestioning obedience to authority in general are scored.

B. Motifs which stress the importance of attending to and conforming to general public opinion or some segment of it are scored.

C. Motifs which elaborate on the importance of respect for or obedience to the law, regulations, or traditional customs of a people are scored. Excluded are general references to patriotism and loyalty to country; but the explicit subordination of self to the good of the country would be scored.

D. Motifs which stress the importance of obedience training in childhood are scored.

E. Motifs which elaborate religious themes — for example, respect for or obedience to God's will — are excluded from scoring.

INDEX

Achievement attitudes: and improved standard of living, 72; in public opinion survey, 69–72; and self-improvement, 70–71; and status mobility hypothesis, 70–72

Achievement motivation: consequences of, 92–94; definition of, 12; determinants of, 14–16; in dream reports, 50–61; and entrepreneurial activity, 16; ethnic variations in, 2–3, 7, 12–16, 50; group differences in, 79–80; and ideology, 15–16; in Nigeria, 7; and population pressure, 82–86; social class differences in, 13; and status mobility hypothesis, 16–21, 57–61; and status mobility patterns, 89–92; and status respect, 4, 87–89; vs. authoritarianism, 80

Achievement values: criteria for scoring, 66, 113–16; examples of, 64–65; in Ibo literature, 76–77; and status mobility, 67–68

Ajayi, J., 38

Atkinson, J., 97

Bacon, M., 19

Barry, H., 19

Bascom, W., 38

Berelson, B., 104

Berlew, D., 96

Biobaku, S., 38

Bradburn, N., 13, 15, 96

Bureaucratic behavior, 6

Caste and class; see Status system

Child, I., 19, 96

Coleman, J., 8, 9, 47, 48, 73, 74, 88

Cooley, W., 110

Dreams: achievement motivation in, 50–61; and daydreams, 52; examples of, 52–56; n Achievement measured in, 52, 95–102; and psycho-cultural lag, 22

Durkheim, E., 10

Economic development: attitudes toward, 71; of Hausa, 73; of Ibo, 73–75; psychological factors in, 1; of Yoruba, 73

Eggan, D., 51

Entrepreneurial activity, 16, 40

Fallers, L., 17

Forde, D., 33, 34, 38

Forrest, D., 52

Free, L., 69, 70

Freud, S., 22, 51, 52

Friedman, G., 96

Galletti, B., 86

Gordon, H., 51

Green, M., 9, 33

Hagen, E., 87, 89

Hall, C., 51

Hausa: economy, 28; nineteenth-century status mobility system, 25–32; politics, 26, 31; religion, 25, 46–47; role in contemporary Nigeria, 7

Horton, W., 82, 83, 85, 86

Ibo: behavioral traits of, 9; contemporary achievement patterns, 73–75; education, 73–74; nineteenth-century status mobility system, 32–37; politics, 32–33, 75–77;